The Seven Ages Of Woman: A Consideration Of The Successive Phases Of Woman's Life

Mary Scharlieb

THE SEVEN AGES
OF WOMAN

A Consideration of the Successive Phases
of Woman's Life

BY

MARY SCHARLIEB, M.D., M.S.Lond.

Vice-President of the Association of Registered Medical Women
Late Senior Surgeon to the New Hospital for Women and Gynaecologist to the
Royal Free Hospital

CASSELL AND COMPANY, LTD
London, New York, Toronto and Melbourne

RA778
S3
1915

First published 1915

PREFACE

THERE are many excellent and some time-honoured manuals for the instruction of young wives and mothers. My intention in writing this little book is not so much to add to their number as to afford a more general guide for women throughout life.

In my humble and no doubt inadequate effort to fulfil a somewhat lofty ambition, I have found it necessary to consider briefly the life of the young girl with reference to her health, management, and education. To this naturally succeed a few chapters of counsel to the young wife and the young mother that will, I hope, be of service to them during a wonderfully interesting but perplexing period of their life.

A remembrance of my own anxieties and perplexities has led to a few chapters concerning the management of children during " the noisy years "; and the constant requests of my patients to tell them where they can get a book in

Preface

which they will find some guidance during and after the climacteric have induced me to add two short chapters on this subject.

Therefore, to my patients, young, middle-aged, and old, I respectfully dedicate this book.

MARY SCHARLIEB

149, HARLEY STREET, W.

CONTENTS

PART I

THE YOUNG GIRL

CHAPTER I

THE YEARS IMMEDIATELY PRECEDING PUBERTY

CHAPTER II

THE PERIOD OF PHYSICAL CHANGE

CHAPTER III

ADVENT OF PUBERTY

Contents

Contents

Contents

Contents

xi

Contents

Contents

CHAPTER III

THE COMMONER AILMENTS OF CHILDHOOD

PART VI

THE WOMAN IN MIDDLE AGE

PART VII

THE WOMAN IN OLD AGE

THE SEVEN AGES OF WOMAN

PART I

THE YOUNG GIRL

CHAPTER I

THE YEARS IMMEDIATELY PRECEDING PUBERTY

IT is impossible to say which period of a woman's life is the most important. As each age comes under consideration one is tempted to say, *This* is the most important period. But the years between absolute childhood and the dawn of adolescence claim a very special attention, because on the management of the child during those years depends in a great measure her fitness for the momentous changes that immediately follow them.

As we shall have occason to point out in a subsequent chapter, the whole human organism is in a constant state of flux and alteration during the years of puberty and adolescence. The few years between the end of childhood and

puberty appear to afford a breathing space intermediate between the rapid growth and development which precede and the still more rapid
growth and development which lie immediately
ahead of them. During these years growth continues, and so, to some extent, does development ;
but, taken as a whole, these are years of consoli-
dation. Upon the successful management of the
pre-pubertal period depends in a great measure
the ability of the girl to endure without injury
the extraordinary up-rush of developmental
energy that will shortly occur. Much has been
written and taught concerning the necessity for
limiting a girl's activities during the trying
years of adolescence ; but it is well to bear in
mind that much can be done by way of preparation to render her organism fit to stand the
strain. The wise mother will endeavour so to
regulate her child's life that it may be adequately
prepared for the difficulties that lie before it.

**Development and growth of the child's
body.**—The child's body during the years immediately before puberty grows steadily, although
with intervals of rest. Growth is in excess of
development, and the child still retains much
of its neutral characteristics. There is relatively
little difference between the boy and the girl at
this time. There is a certain angularity and
sometimes a lankiness of appearance ; it is perhaps not a very prepossessing age, for the girl

has lost the rounded outline and charm of infancy, and has not yet acquired the still greater charm of adolescence.

The task of the mother or guardian during these years is chiefly one of preparation, of laying a really solid foundation of health that will stand the child in good stead later on. In order that she should be able to fulfil her duty she ought to know something of the structure and functions of the child's body. The mother must remember that her developing children are neither magnified babies nor small adults. If the photograph of a normal baby were enlarged to the same size as the photograph of a child of 10 or 12, and, still more, if it were compared with the photograph of a young adult, it would be seen at once that the powers of Nature secure not only growth in size, but a very noticeable alteration in shape and proportion. These changes in the structure and appearance of the child's body will be considered in detail in the next chapter. For the moment it is sufficient to remember that, great as are the changes during the years immediately preceding puberty, they are yet only the commencement of the transformation scene.

Intellectual and spiritual development.— Spiritually and intellectually much the same quiet growth and development are occurring. The intellect becomes stronger, more able to fathom the meaning and import of what is learnt, but there is as yet no marvellous display of extra power; that is reserved for the next stage. The girl still resembles her brother, not only in body, but also in mind and in general outlook on life. If she has been favoured both by heredity and by environment, she is at this stage perfectly frank and open, there are no concealments, and although affection may be warm and deep, the mirror of the mind is as yet undimmed by the breath of passion. There is probably little appreciation of the beauties of scenery, and little or no love of art. Here and there an exceptional child shows a distinct gift for music, drawing, or other forms of art, but the whole outlook is calm, quiet; in a word, the child is matter-of-fact, and the mother or guardian has a comparatively easy time in dealing with a nature that still retains much of the simplicity of childhood.

The great duty of the mother during these preparatory years is to assist her child's organism to gather strength and to collect material ready for the next stage. Spiritually she will find that in most instances the young girl at this period retains the simple, unquestioning faith of the little child; there is little or no questioning as to the why and wherefore of the facts that she is taught, and still less is there self-consciousness or introspection. One of the differences between the years immediately preceding puberty and the period of adolescence which follows is that in the former period the mother can see into her child's mind, while the child herself sees very little ; whereas later on the youthful personality becomes intensely self-conscious, and is at the same time more or less completely hidden, even from the mother's sympathetic eye.

There are those who would have us believe that sexual feelings and sex consciousness develop at a very early age. In abnormal children, no doubt, this may be the case ; but in the healthy child who has been well brought up, sex feelings and consciousness are dormant, if not absent, and boys and girls will associate with each other, confide in each other, and behave generally in a way that would be absolutely impossible after the great awakening.

This neutrality of soul and spirit, this want of self-consciousness, is the great justification for those authorities who approve and practise co-education of boys and girls. There is just sufficient sex difference to make the boy and girl mutually stimulating and therefore mutually helpful from an educational point of view. Exceptions will, of course, be found to this rule, but they are exceptions, and therefore do not necessarily affect the management of children in the pre-adolescent years.

CHAPTER II

THE PERIOD OF PHYSICAL CHANGE

Changes in the skeleton.—During the pubertal and adolescent years the changes in the skeleton are so well marked and rapid that they cannot fail to attract the attention of all who are in contact with the young; and yet it is a curious fact that the phenomenon which appeals most to the ordinary onlooker is the increase in the length of the bones, whereas the most striking change in the skeleton is really the difference of proportion between the head and body of the young adult and the head and body of the little child. The head grows but little after the end of absolute childhood, and does not assume the adult proportion of being about one-twelfth of the total length of the body until growth is finished. If the adult head had grown in proportion to the size that it was in infancy, the effect would be positively grotesque. Holiday after holiday one hears the remark addressed to the adolescent girl, " Why, how you have grown—two or three inches at least ! " And thus the wonderful change is exaggerated. It is true that the rate of growth during adoles-

6

cence is very great, but the changes in proportion
and in moulding are greater still.

In the girl the most wonderful changes occur
in the pelvis. During childhood and early youth
the bones of the pelvis and its angle to the
horizon are much the same in both sexes, but at
the time of puberty great changes occur, the
girl's pelvic bones become relatively lighter,
thinner, and more graceful. The upper part of
the ilium (hip-bone) expands, and instead of
its surfaces facing forwards they tend to face
each other. This change gives width to the
pelvis. At the same time the diameters of the
pelvic brim change. In the male throughout
life, and in the female up to puberty, the
diameter from front to back is approximately
the same as the diameter from side to side,
but in the female from puberty onwards the
latter diameter is markedly the longer. The
cavity of the pelvis also enlarges absolutely
and relatively, and the pubic arch becomes
wider, having approximately the value of the
right angle, whereas in the child and in the
male this angle is somewhere about 60° to 70°.
These changes are to a certain extent due to the
innate tendency of the bones so to develop, but
that they are chiefly due to the great developmental changes in the contained organs, the
womb and its appendages, is proved by the fact
that where these organs are virtually absent or

badly developed the female pelvis fails to undergo the perfect metamorphosis, and remains throughout life more or less masculine in type.

Another skeletal change of interest is that the spinal column acquires its adult curves — much more marked in the female than in the male. The angle formed at the junction of the spine with the sacrum increases, and so too does the inclination of the pelvic brim to the horizon. All these changes in the female spine and pelvis have for their object the facilitation of pregnancy and parturition, the head of the normal human infant fitting the normal adult female pelvis as accurately as the hand fits the glove.

In consequence of the increased width of the pelvis the heads of the femora (thigh bones) are carried farther out, their necks become more oblique, and a greater width is obtained between the upper extremities of these bones. The knees, however, in the erect position remain in contact, and consequently the whole length of the woman's thigh bone slopes from above downwards and inwards. To this must be ascribed the typical feminine gait, which has a grace of its own, but which, if exaggerated, may lead to an undue roll, or even a waddle.

The muscles also undergo typical changes, those around the hip becoming relatively more developed than do those of the male. This, again, increases the comparative heaviness and

8

massiveness of the lower part of the female figure.

In addition to these changes in the bones of the skeleton and in the muscles, the girl, as adolescence progresses, tends to develop a certain amount of fat. In normal cases this is only sufficient to add to the beauty of the body, substituting soft curves and graceful outlines for the squareness and angularity of the male.

Changes in the organs.—Among the most obvious outward changes in the organs of the adolescent girl is the development of the breast. From birth up to puberty the breasts of the boy and girl remain flat, small, and undeveloped, but at the advent of puberty the girl's bust undergoes a great change. The gland itself increases not only in size, but also in complexity of structure. In many instances this true development is made to appear more marked than it really is, partly by the development of a certain amount of fat, and partly by the increase of size in the large chest muscles which throw the gland into greater prominence. The nipple, with its areola of delicately coloured tissue, becomes more obvious, and it is evident from the alterations in structure and appearance of the girl's body that the momentous change has been accomplished, and that we have before us a potential mother.

The internal changes in organs which cannot

9

be seen during life are also marvellous. The womb, which had grown but little since infancy, and which had but a languid circulation, becomes larger, plumper, more richly supplied with blood, and its body—the part which is being prepared for the eventual conception of an infant—becomes larger in proportion to the neck, which had hitherto been its equal in length. The ovaries also undergo growth and development; some of the primitive ovules enlarge, and in doing so begin to protrude a little from the general surface of the organ. One of them becomes fully ripe every twenty-eight days, is seized in the fringed extremity of the oviduct, and bursts, the contained germ cell passing along the tube into the uterus. The mucous membrane of the uterus, in sympathy with these ovarian changes, becomes greatly congested, and relief ensues with the occurrence of the periodic discharge—*menstruation*.

Changes in personal appearance.—In addition to the development of the bust and hips, a very considerable change occurs in the young girl's appearance. The hair becomes brighter in hue, glossier, and possibly more disposed to curl. The complexion clears and brightens, adding greatly to personal charm, while the eyes acquire a brightness and increased depth of expression which indicate the subtle changes occurring in the soul and spirit.

CHAPTER III

ADVENT OF PUBERTY

As the word *puberty* implies, this time of life is associated with an increase in the growth of hair. Especially is this noticeable on the mons veneris and about the vulva, and in the axillæ or armpits; and together with the growth of hair comes the development in the skin of certain glands which secrete a somewhat oily material which is perfectly natural and healthy, but which necessitates a strict attention to cleanliness and a free use of a non-perfumed and non-irritating soap, such, for instance, as Castile soap or olive oil soap. This appearance of hair, taken in conjunction with possibly a colourless discharge and the other changes described in the last chapter, should give the girl's mother ample warning that menstruation is imminent. She ought to tell her daughter what to expect, otherwise the girl may suffer a considerable nervous shock when the great event occurs. Much of a girl's happiness and health depends on her understanding the import of the changes that are occurring in her body. If she unfortunately believes that menstruation and its attendant phenomena are signs of illness, and if she is encouraged to treat them as if they were abnormalities, the foundation of nervous ill-health is likely to be laid. If, on the other hand, she is taught that these changes are beneficent, that they are necessary to her full development of womanhood, and that indeed they are the promise that after a few years she will be fit to receive the great crown and joy of a woman's life, motherhood, she will then view her condition not only with patience, but also with joy. The motherly instinct is deeply implanted in every young girl, and she will be willing, if necessary, to suffer restrictions on present enjoyment and activities in order that the change in her constitution may be satisfactorily accomplished, and that her health may be so well established as to enable her to play her part in life to the greatest advantage. The girl ought to be warned that some day she will find that she has a discharge of blood, or of blood-stained fluid, from the vagina, and that this discharge may be accompanied by feelings of lassitude and heaviness, by discomfort, and perhaps by pain. She must also be told that the amount and the duration of the discharge are uncertain. In these matters each girl and woman is a law unto herself, and equally good health may be maintained whether the monthly discharge (the *period*, as it is generally called) lasts three days or 'seven days, and whether the number of sanitary towels used daily during the first few days be two — the least demanded by decency and comfort — or three. The total number of diapers or sanitary towels that may be needed varies much, but probably any number under eight may be considered to denote scantiness, and any number over twelve profuseness of the discharge. These criteria are, of course, very rough, but they are sufficient to prevent girls who use half a dozen diapers from fearing that they are having a flooding, and, on the other hand, they would indicate to those who are using forty or more diapers that they need not desire medicine to increase the flow.*

A girl must also be warned that a certain amount of flow is especially likely to occur when she first rises from bed. Owing to partial closure of the vagina by the fold of mucous membrane termed the hymen, the discharge collects in the passage during the night and passes away when the erect position is assumed or the first urine is passed. The natural interval between the periods — that is to say, the time between the commencement of one period and the commencement of the next — is twenty-eight days; that is, a lunar month, hence the word *menstruation.* But it is not to be considered

---

* Cases illustrative of these two errors were seen by me in one afternoon at the New Hospital for Women, Euston Road.

13

abnormal or a sign of disease if there is some little deviation from this rule. The antedating or postponing of the period by two or three days does not constitute an irregularity.

Some mothers, and still more naturally some children, are very much perturbed if menstruation, after having occurred once, does not immediately become regular. It is, however, quite common for a girl to have a period, and then to see nothing more for six months or a year. This is especially likely to be the case when menstruation has commenced very early—for instance, at 11 or 12 years of age. Far from being a bad sign and indicating ill health, it is really better for so young a girl if the discharge occurs at longer intervals. Further than this, the first few periods are not to be taken as typical of the individual girl's future menstruation; they may be longer or shorter, scantier or more profuse, at first, but after a time the function settles down and each woman establishes a rule for herself. It is only after the rule has become established that greater or less frequency, and more or less flow, can be considered to be abnormal for the individual.

It is also necessary to impress on mothers and children that pain, or the capacity for bearing pain, varies largely, and that whereas some young girls make light of the natural congestion and discomfort, others, with an unfortunate capacity for appreciating pain, will consider the same amount of inconvenience to be a veritable illness. Undoubtedly pain varies in intensity, just as does the capacity for bearing it ; but, as a rule, in healthy girls under favourable circumstances neither the pain nor the discharge itself is sufficient to justify withdrawal from the usual duties and pleasures of life. The wise mother should know how to shield her child from undue exertion without making a monthly illness out of a natural function, and so setting up a false standard of health and disease in the mind of the inexperienced adolescent.

It should be easy to arrange that extra long walks, strenuous exercises, games, and dancing should be put aside during the first few days of each period; but in the case of the healthy girl it is most undesirable that too great a difference should be made in her life's routine, and that her own attention and that of her friends should be repeatedly drawn to what, after all, is a normal function. As a rule, it will be found that after a few years, when the function is thoroughly established, the young woman will be able to do very much as usual, and will not need to make any special arrangements for a few days monthly.

CHAPTER IV

ABNORMALITIES OF MENSTRUATION

Amenorrhœa, or absence of menstruation.—
The menstrual function may never develop, or,
having developed, it may subsequently lapse.
The causes of primary amenorrhœa, the variety
in which menstruation has never developed, may
be due to some deformity of structure in the
generative organs or to a defect in the nervous
mechanism. It is perfectly evident that if any
of the organs concerned in the function of menstruation be absent or seriously defective, its
phenomena will also be absent. There are cases,
happily rare, in which there is a congenital absence of the ovaries, tubes, or uterus. It is very
unusual for these organs to be entirely absent;
even in extreme cases some vestige of them is
generally to be found. Much more frequently,
primitive amenorrhœa is to be found in the case
of girls who have altogether failed to undergo
the usual developmental changes. In such subjects the breasts remain infantile, the pubes
and axillæ have little or no hair, and the parts
of the vulva resemble those of children of 10
or 12 years of age. The internal organs like-

wise fail to develop, and the uterus may be found to be small, thin, flat, and with a mucous membrane showing no signs of preparation for function. In such cases little can be done, but an attempt should be made by the administration of suitable drugs, by prolonged treatment with electricity, and by nourishing and stimulating food, to assist the arrested development.

Occult menstruation. — These cases resemble primitive amenorrhœa in the fact that no discharge has appeared, but the girls are often strong and well developed. The uterus and ovaries are well formed, and the nervous stimulation is perfect. The trouble is that there is some impediment to the exit of the menstrual fluid. Possibly the hymen is *imperforate*—that is to say, it has no opening—or some obstruction may exist in the vagina or uterus. In such cases the girl probably has all the symptoms of menstruation, and, indeed, a considerable amount of distress at regular monthly intervals, but she lacks the relief of the discharge. The abdomen slowly enlarges until a more or less considerable swelling may be felt in the lower part. In all such cases professional advice should be procured, and in almost all relief is safe and easy.

Secondary amenorrhœa. —The usual phenomena of puberty may have occurred, the periods have been established, and have been regular for a time, sometimes for years. Then, either gradually or perhaps suddenly, menstruation ceases, and both the girl and her mother will be very anxious to know what is the cause, and whether it is remediable. There have been many old superstitions with regard to the absence of menstruation, and in many instances it is attributed to chill or over-fatigue of mind or body. If the chill be so serious as to endanger the general health or to permit of the development of serious disease, such as tuberculosis, then amenorrhœa may follow the chill, but it will be due to the disease, inflammatory, tubercular, etc., and not directly to the chill itself. Amenorrhœa is one of the symptoms of early phthisis, and therefore deserves immediate and careful attention; but it is always to be remembered that it is the phthisis, or other tubercular manifestation, that must be treated, and that if and when health returns the monthly function will return with it.

Amenorrhœa of longer or shorter duration may also follow other exhausting diseases, such as the various infectious fevers, acute rheumatism, and operations, e.g. that for appendicitis. In all these cases the same rule holds good — restore the patient's general health and menstruation will reappear.

Another cause of amenorrhœa is mental disorder. Not infrequently anxious mothers or other friends represent to the doctor that the

patient is mentally ill, or is suffering from neuras-
thenia, because her periods have ceased. The
same fallacy exists in these sad cases. The
period ceases to appear because the nervous
mechanism is disordered. Restore the general
nutrition and the mental balance, and the period
will return.

Anæmia is a very common cause of amenorrhœa, and here it must be looked upon as an
effort of Nature to arrest or to minimise the
expenditure of a bankrupt state. There is
already too little red blood in the body, and
if the usual monthly loss occurred the anæmia
would be increased, therefore the whole attention
of doctor and friends should be devoted to the
cure of the anæmia. An open-air life, plenty
of nourishing food (especially plenty of milk),
absence of fatigue and worry, change of air, sea-
bathing, and the administration of iron and
arsenic, should be carefully and vigorously employed. When the anæmia is cured the amenorrhœa will be cured also.

Abnormalities of quantity.—In many of
the states above mentioned the periods may be
insufficient but not entirely absent, and the same
remarks as to causation and treatment would
apply. On the other hand, the period may be
in excess, coming too frequently (*metrorrhagia*),
or too profusely (*menorrhagia*). These abnormalities naturally excite considerable anxiety,

and it is always well when possible to consult the family doctor. It is, however, necessary to bear in mind that until the individual's rule is established there may be several abundant periods, but that when the function is really established the amount will probably become normal. In cases where the flow continues to be too frequent in occurrence or excessive in amount advice must be sought, for it is the doctor only who can say whether the symptoms are due to some structural change or whether the error is purely functional. It is to be remembered that generally the doctor will be unable to give a reliable opinion without internal examination, and that in the case of a young girl it is very undesirable to do this except under a general anæsthetic. Not only are the parts undeveloped and an examination would probably be both painful and incomplete, but also the whole proceeding is extremely distasteful to a young girl, and is apt to cause a certain amount of nervous shock and mental distress. The necessary examination lasts but a few minutes, and can generally be carried out under gas ; it is then much less distressing than the extraction of a tooth, for no sore cavity or aching jaw is left to cause subsequent pain.

Irregularity. — In some instances the period is quite sufficient, and when it comes is normal in all respects, but it does not come regularly.

Abnormalities of Menstruation

It may be absent for six weeks or even for two or three months, and then again it may come too frequently two or three times in succession. If this occurs shortly after puberty no heed should be taken, but if it occurs after the girl's type of menstruation is established there is probably some definite cause for the aberration. In many instances it will be found that too much has been undertaken, and that there has been too much strain owing to excess of intellectual work, especially when accompanied by ambition or anxiety, or the girl may be suffering from an over-devotion to athletics, especially when she plays hockey, basket ball, or other team games for her school. Girls are far more prone than boys to a spirit of ambition and emulation, which may be individualistic or corporate. In the one case the girl is anxious for her own reputation ; in the other, for the reputation of her school. The effect, however, is the same, and owing to the combined overstrain of body and mind a condition of lassitude and perhaps anæmia supervenes, and then the periods become irregular.

Painful periods. —Many young girls suffer from *dysmenorrhœa*, or painful menstruation. As a rule the function begins painlessly, but after a time, owing to internal congestion, which may be the result of chills or constipation, the period becomes slowly but persistently less comfortable until it is always accompanied by backache, abdominal pain, and a sense of weight and dragging. Even if untreated this condition tends to wear out, and it is comparatively rare to find women suffering much from this type of dysmenorrhœa after the age of 25 to 30, even if still unmarried.

Another form of dysmenorrhœa is caused — or at any rate is accompanied by —displacement of the womb. These displacements of the organ are usually backward, and are known as *retroversion* (backward turning), or *retroflexion* (backward bending). In some instances displacement, more especially the retroflexion, seems to have existed from childhood, perhaps from birth ; it is then due to a congenital deformity of the womb, and is difficult to remedy. In the majority of cases displacements are caused either gradually by prolonged congestion, which renders the uterus top-heavy, by an habitually over-full bladder, which pushes it back, or by constipation, which has much the same effect. Some cases of backward displacement are, however, more acute. They may then be caused by such accidents as over-jumping, as from a wall or similar height, or by falls in riding, dancing, or skating. In such cases the patient can generally recall when the pain began, and can sometimes remember a probable cause.

Some doctors are quite certain that no displacement of the womb causes dysmenorrhœa, but whether the pain be due to displacement, to the accompanying congestion, or to psychic causes, the fact remains that the replacement of the organ under an anæsthetic, and the introduction of a pessary to hold it in place for a few months, will nearly always cure the patient, unless the nervous element is very strong.

There are many other causes of painful menstruation, among them neuralgia and rheumatism Each case should be carefully treated on its own merits, and the patient should always be encouraged to hope for the relief which is nearly sure to come.

Membranous dysmenorrhœa. — There is a small but not insignificant group of cases in which the pain amounts to absolute agony. It is often due to the casting off of the lining membrane of the uterus in a more or less complete form. The membrane is rolled into a ball by the action of the uterus, and is then expelled through the narrow, undilated neck of that organ. The pain accompanying this procedure is very great, and strongly resembles that of early miscarriage. It comes on in paroxysms, and is generally accompanied by nausea, vomiting, possibly fainting, and diarrhœa. It is no exaggeration to call this an illness. The agony of pain due to the expulsion probably lasts three or four hours only, but the patient is generally much exhausted and very much upset in mind by what very naturally seems to her an alarming state of health. As a matter of fact there is no danger, but the inconvenience is great. In all such cases a doctor should be consulted, and probably a small operation will bring about a cure.

CHAPTER V

DOMESTIC CARE OF THE YOUNG GIRL

FROM all that has gone before it is quite evident that the whole nature of the adolescent girl is in a highly unstable condition, that every part of her organism is growing, developing, changing, at so rapid a rate, that the normal is always verging on the abnormal, and that a slight excess in any part of the movement is likely to lead to disaster. The wise and successful management of this stage of a young girl's life calls for knowledge, foresight, prudence, and sympathy on the part of those who have her in their keeping. Alas, it is but few women who have made a sufficient study of the peculiarities of adolescence, and who are prepared to deal wisely and well with the highly sensitive and unstable organism confided to them. The wealth of change and the rapidity of growth described in the young girl have no doubt their counterpart in similar changes in the young of other animals, but the intellectual and spiritual development is not only out of all proportion to such changes as occur in the brute creation, but is also the delicately adjusted pivot on which all other changes turn. The more complex and the more delicate the machine, the more readily is it put out of gear, and the greater the knowledge and experience that are needed in order that it should produce the best work of which it is capable. Is it not, therefore, a lamentable fact that many mothers and guardians receive little training, and consequently have but little knowledge to help them in the management of the complicated and highly vitalised machine for which they are responsible?

It may be urged that the world has been going on for a good many thousands of years, that every generation has brought its quota of adolescent girls, and that during all this time but little harm seems to have been done. Yet reflection and knowledge and a consideration of the past, even a remembrance of one's own young days, should suffice to convince us that harm has been done and still is being done. Why are so many young lives cut short? Why do so many fail to come to perfection? Why are so many bent and deformed in some part of their nature? The records of home life and of school life abound with the sad histories of what might have been. Probably the girls that we know represent more or less the survival of the fittest, but there should have been many more, and those who remain to us ought to stand on a higher plane than they do.

Domestic Care of the Young Girl

Food.—The first necessity of all organisms is food. No animal or vegetable can long survive without food that is suitable in quantity and in quality. In considering the provision of food for our children we immediately come on one of the weak points of our nation. It is quite possible that the French housewife has not a superior scientific training in cooking, but at any rate she is vastly superior in the matter of instinct; she is as thrifty as the Scottish housewife, and her cooking is far more appetising. The body needs a sufficient supply of the different kinds of food—proteins, carbohydrates, hydrocarbons, and salts.

One fundamental error that is very generally made with regard to proteid or flesh-forming foods is the undue importance that is ascribed to meat. Meat, especially the prime cuts of meat such as are expected on the tables of the well-to-do, is costly, and it would tend greatly to the advantage of the nation if our housewives were to recognise more freely the value of other proteins, such as cheese, peas, beans, lentils, and nuts. If an adequate use were made of these articles of diet a much smaller quantity of flesh food would suffice, and it would be found that the less expensive varieties of meat would suffice to give the flavour and the nourishment that are to be found in the many savoury stews, soups, and other con-

coctions met with among the poorer orders in
France. A typical meal ought to consist of all
the chief food stuffs in due proportion, and
it is of the first importance to the growing girl
that her food should not only be sufficient in
quantity and well considered in quality, but also
varied and made palatable by due admixture
and by clever cooking. Adolescent girls, as a
rule, go to school daily, and if they are boarders
they have to prepare for hours of steady work ;
it is therefore of extreme importance that they
should be down in good time for breakfast in
order to have leisure for a sufficient meal, and
that the meal itself should be so well prepared
and so well chosen as to secure the fulfilment
of its object. The meal should consist of some
cereal preparation, such as oatmeal porridge,
Quaker Oats, Shredded Wheat, Force or Grape
Nuts, together with half a pint of milk and
some sweetening agent such as golden syrup,
sugar, or marmalade. To this may be added
an egg, a rasher of bacon, or fish, with brown
bread and butter, and half a pint of coffee made
with milk. In such a meal all the necessary
elements of a good diet are represented ; there
is plenty of protein in the cereal as well as in
the other articles suggested ; the carbohydrates
or starches are contained in the cereals, the
bread, and the sugar ; the hydrocarbons or fats
are present in the butter, milk, cream, and

fat of the bacon; while the salts are fairly dis-
tributed.

After such a breakfast no harm will be
done even to the rapidly growing girl if one of
the two other chief meals of the day should
consist of bread and butter, cheese, fruit, and
milk. Dinner, whether taken in the middle of
the day, or in the evening when the work is
done, may consist of soup, followed by fish,
meat, or poultry, with potatoes and green vegetables, and as a final course sweets, or fruit and
cream. A cup of tea may be allowed in the
afternoon, but its stimulating and exciting effect
make it unsuitable for any prominent place in
the dietary of the young girl.

It is hardly necessary to say that, unless
given by a doctor's orders, all forms of alcohol
are unsuited for an adolescent. Young people
need food to enable them to form the rapidly
growing tissues of their bodies and to restore
those portions which are broken up and burnt
during their constant and sometimes excessive
activities. That is to say, the fires of their life
need stoking with good, sound fuel, but they do
not need stimulating as one would stimulate a
dull fire by dipping the fuel in paraffin or spirit.
Combustion is quite sufficiently rapid in young
people, and needs no artificial encouragement.

When possible, the chief meal should be taken
in the middle of the day, or at any rate some hours

before bedtime. Digestion is slow or even suspended during sleep, and a full meal taken just before bedtime is likely to remain in the stomach undigested, or partially digested, and therefore to interfere with sleep.

Exercise.—Exercise is a subject which demands very careful consideration. Healthy young people, as a rule, take quite sufficient voluntarily, but there are adolescents—especially adolescent girls—who appear to be indolent and to prefer lying about, or lounging, book in hand, to taking the active exercise which they really need. Such children need to be directed, and it is partly with this object in view that games mistresses are now appointed in all large schools.

Team games are valuable not only for their physical, but also for their moral effects. In games such as cricket, hockey, golf, and basket ball every part of the girl's frame is educated and developed ; her eye is trained, and every muscle works in co-ordination with others. Nor is this physical development the whole of the benefit received. Team games are admirable in their discipline of the moral nature ; they teach promptness to obey, readiness to subordinate the advantage of the individual to the profit of the team ; they also teach invaluable lessons as to command. The captain of a team soon learns that merely issuing orders will not secure success. She finds that tyranny, prejudice, and favouritism are absolutely fatal to the proper *esprit de corps* and to the *moral* of those she wishes to lead to victory. If she be worthy of her position she quickly learns that courtesy and consideration are as essential to success as is the power to judge character, and to set each member of her team to the task for which the individual is best fitted.

Team games are so important, both in their power to promote bodily efficiency and to secure the development of character, that one recognises the profundity of wisdom that led the great Duke of Wellington to say that the Battle of Waterloo was won on the playing fields of Eton.

Team games, however, are not the only form of exercise desirable for adolescent girls. A certain proportion of time—half an hour a day, or an hour three times a week—should be devoted to Swedish exercises. These exercises appear to excel all others because they are carefully planned to call into play pretty nearly every organ of the human body, and also because in each well-considered scheme of Swedish exercises there is a gradual *increase* in the output of exertion up to a certain point, and then a gradual *decrease*, until at the end of the selected group of exercises the body returns to rest. At the present time there is no difficulty in obtaining thoroughly well-trained Englishwomen to teach these exercises, and a serious effort should be made to secure the introduction of this health-giving agency into all our schools. Scandinavian children hold themselves better, walk better, and sit better than do the children of other European nations, and this superiority is certainly due to the universal adoption of suitable gymnastics.

It is possible that an exclusive devotion to gymnastic exercises might tend to produce a certain angularity in young girls, but the antidote to this is to be found in games and also in dancing. Dancing, properly taught and properly executed, should lead to the natural assumption of beautiful positions and to the possession of elastic and graceful movements. Girls who enjoy the advantages of training in exercises, games, and dancing ought never to slouch, never to stand or sit awkwardly, and should be strong, active, and graceful.

The old-fashioned stereotyped walk in what girls call " a crocodile " is one of the worst forms of exercise possible ; physically it is wearisome, and morally it fails to develop the qualities that are essential for success in life. The girls walk two and two ; there is nothing to relieve the monotony of the exercise, and, still worse, there is nothing to check silly chatter and unkind gossip. During these walks the foundations are laid for the exclusive and undesirable friendships into which girls are so apt to fall, and an opportunity is given for the exchange of confidences which are always futile and sometimes positively deleterious.

Rest and sleep.—There is no doubt that in most of our schools, and also in many homes, the time allotted to sleep is altogether insufficient in the case of the rapidly growing and developing adolescent. Some years ago Miss Alice Ravenhill made a careful inquiry into the amount of sleep taken by girls under many different conditions in England. In the great majority of instances she found that the hours of sleep were much too short, and that a really adequate amount of sleep was altogether exceptional. Adolescents need ten hours' sleep as compared with the twelve hours required by the child and the eight hours which ought to be secured by the adult. In order that young girls should have this necessary rest for both brain and body they ought to be in bed before 9 P.M. and should not get up before 7 A.M. Against this salutary rule young girls are very apt to rebel; they argue that their preparation for the lessons of the next day demands that they should sit up much longer, and sometimes they plead that they work so hard all day that they ought to be allowed to read or otherwise amuse themselves for an hour before going to bed. Probably real diligence earlier in the evening would not only enable the work to be done to time, but might also secure the coveted relaxation.

With regard to rest other than sleep, it is most desirable that a break should be made in the middle of the morning and another in the middle of the afternoon, but in the case of most healthy young girls a judicious ordering of the time-table, so that exercises, games, or dancing shall be interspersed with the more purely intellectual work, suffices to give the necessary refreshment, and to avoid prolonged sitting or standing, which are in themselves irksome to healthy young creatures.

Clothing. — The adolescent girl's clothing needs very careful consideration. In principle it should be light, loose, and comfortable. There should be no pressure anywhere, and the less the garments " fit " the better will they mould themselves to the growing, developing, altering figure of the wearer. Anything in the nature of ordinary corsets is quite unsuitable ; if they are tight they tend to check the natural development of hip and bust ; if, on the other hand, they are loose, they are at once uncomfortable, useless, and unsightly. The hygienic bodice, made of stitched jean furnished with shoulder-straps, can be adapted so as to remove all pressure from the hips and waist, and to it can be fastened knickers and skirt, so that the weight of these garments hangs from the shoulders.

Domestic Care of the Young Girl

The stockings should be of cashmere, thinner for summer than for winter, but not transparent ; the shoes should be sufficiently long, and wide enough not to cramp the toes; the heels should not exceed three-quarters of an inch in height and should be broad enough to give firm support to the foot; too high a heel destroys the arch of the foot, and causes undue fatigue, because the tread is never flat, and the wearer of such shoes is always more or less on tiptoe.

The garments should be few as well as simple. Next to the skin a woollen combination, thin in summer and pleasantly substantial in winter ; this garment should be high to the neck and long enough to cover the knees and to come well below the elbow. It is a great safeguard against chill when the wearer is heated by exertion. The knickers should be sufficiently large to secure freedom of action, and should be of woollen material in the winter, and cotton, alpaca, or silk in the summer.

Young girls with short skirts may wear petticoats or dispense with them, according to the season of the year and varying circumstances ; they are always out of place in the gymnasium or when playing games, but will be a comfort in cold and windy weather. They are, of course, also necessary when the skirt of the dress is thin or transparent.

CHAPTER VI

EDUCATION, AND CHOICE OF A PROFESSION

In this chapter we are to consider education in the limited sense of that preparation for the work of life which is carried on during what is popularly known as "schooldays." This explanation is necessary because education in the true sense begins before birth, lasts as long as life endures, and, we have good reason to believe, continues beyond the grave.

The word *education* is frequently misunderstood. Many people imagine that by education is meant the mere process of storing the mind with facts and explanations, whereas both the etymological and the true inward meaning of education is the *leading forth* of latent powers and the development of the same. Education, therefore, concerns not only the mind but the whole being. For the moment, however, we will consider the difficult question that presents itself to parents and to guardians as to how they may best draw out and develop the powers of the young people committed to their care.

Home or school education.—The question at once arises, Shall the girl be educated at home

Education

or at school, and, should the choice be made
that she is to be educated at school, shall she
be sent to boarding-school or day school? The
subject bristles with difficulties. Parents have
very naturally strong views of their own, and,
as a rule, they are little disposed to act upon
advice, although they are eager to ask for it.

It must in fairness be conceded that each
plan of education offers certain advantages. On
the one hand, the mother who determines to
keep her child at home retains within her own
grasp the possibility of watching, restraining,
and fostering the moral tendencies of her child.
She is able also to give the girl the opportunity
of learning a certain amount of household management and domestic economy as well as
the ordinary subjects of a liberal education.
This is certainly a great advantage. The girl also
leads a more sheltered life, and is more protected
from infection, morally as well as physically.
The mother is able to choose her companions
and to regulate her studies and amusements.

On the other hand, the home-bred girl
misses advantages which, one would think, far
outweigh those that are to be secured by education at home. The girl who goes to boarding-
school and is quite away from her home for the
working terms of the year is really meeting
under specially favourable circumstances the
world in which she must eventually live and

work; she is an individual unit in an organised society, she is a member of a real community, her position in the community and her personal value as a member of the society depend upon her conduct. Her father's wealth, her mother's position in society, are scarcely known to her schoolfellows, and do not weigh with them at all. What the girl *is*, or what she may *become*, determines her value in the school. This is an excellent preparation for adult life, a real development of the faculties and gifts that will be of value hereafter.

Another valuable asset in school life is that each girl and her conduct stand at the bar of the public opinion of the school. The young are merciless critics of each other; the smallest dereliction from their code of honour is viewed with disgust, and is punished with the utmost rigour of the unwritten law of the school. It is true that the code of honour accepted by school girls is a law unto itself, but with all its peculiarities it presents a very fair standard by which to live, and, on the whole, is justly comparable to that extraordinary, but in the result satisfactory, code which makes the English public school boy the worthy father of the best type of Englishman.

So much for the discipline which the girls receive from each other, but above and beyond this there are the rules, written and unwritten, of the school, the discipline which represents the law of the State, and has nothing above it save and except only the sanction of Divine Law. The question of school discipline is exceptionally important and difficult; it presents a problem that every headmaster and headmistress has to solve to the best of his or her ability. Such questions as the following arise : Shall there be much, and careful, inspection and guidance by the masters and mistresses of the school, or shall the young people be largely left to govern themselves, their own sense of honour acting as inspector, and their own capacity for obedience securing their safety ? On the whole, the great schools of England, whether for boys or for girls, have elected in favour of trusting to the honour of the young people. Not that each individual does what is right in his or her own eyes, but that the authority is delegated to chosen members of the community, and that discipline is enforced through prefects, monitors, and similar officers. Here, again, the analogy of school life with adult life is very close, and is no doubt entirely to the advantage of the community. But just as in the life of the State certain qualities are necessary in those who guide its destinies, so in the successful school the officers of the miniature state must be individuals conspicuous for truth, honour, obedience, for power of sympathy, and for capacity to govern.

The Seven Ages of Woman

A third advantage of school life is that of emulation. Many girls who would fail to put forth their best powers if working alone will be stimulated to exertion by the example of their friends and companions. It is to be confessed that with girls emulation is not an unmixed good. Among the smaller natures emulation is apt to foster too great a desire for individual distinction and glory. In some schools prizes and distinctions are awarded to classes or divisions and not to individual students. Such an arrangement makes the best use of the principle of emulation without fostering the ever-present disadvantage of undue individualism and selfishness. The exaggerated influence of emulation, as is remarked elsewhere, is much more evident among girls than boys. Probably this is due to the fact that generations of women have lived and worked without the broadening and strengthening influences which have tended to correct selfishness and too great a love of personal glory in the case of boys and men.

In connection with this we must remember the invaluable quality of *esprit de corps*. It is this which nerves a regiment to attempt the apparently impossible, which secures an abundance of volunteers for every forlorn hope, and which leads public school boys in after life to avoid the evil and to embrace the difficult but necessary good for the honour of their old school.

Education

The name and the reputation of Eton and of Harrow, of Marlborough and of Winchester, and of our other public schools have kept " the soldier firm, the statesman pure," and have contributed more than any influence, except that of religion, to the moulding of our national character. This invaluable quality has to some extent been wanting in girls' schools. The sense of corporate unity and that mysterious idealisation and personification which cause the population of so many square miles to regard itself as an individual nation are gradually, however, permeating our schools for girls, and leading them also to become real entities capable of kindling the enthusiasm of their alumni and of stamping on their plastic minds the image of a soul-mother to be feared, to be loved, and to be cherished throughout life.

In addition to these most important advantages secured to girls at school, it is to be remembered that the same influences will tend to make of the masters and mistresses not merely so many individual educational machines, but a veritable " band of brothers." No school can be successful unless the teachers stand towards the headmistress on the one hand, and the children on the other, in the same relation as do the company officers of a regiment towards their colonel and their men ; they also must be deeply imbued with the *esprit de corps.* The school must be at once their mother, their child, and their lover, the supreme earthly preoccupation of their lives. The school must be their fount of inspiration, its welfare must be the goal to obtain which they are willing " to shun delights and live laborious days."

Another great advantage of school education as compared with working at home is the fact that all the members of the school community are working together for one end —the fitting of the girls to play their part in life. In the home there are many distracting and competing, if not conflicting, interests, and it is extremely difficult both for parents and for children to acquiesce in the young people living within the pale of home life and yet not of it. The temptation is great for the mother to break in on the schoolroom routine and to take her child to certain suitable entertainments, to invade the hours consecrated to study by insisting on the girl fulfilling various social engagements. With all the best will in the world it is scarcely possible for both mother and daughters to carry out an intact programme of school work and to respect the time-table of studies and recreations, and even should their virtue be sufficiently Spartan for this, yet, as said before, the atmosphere of home differs from the atmosphere of school in that the interests of the community cannot fail to be mixed and varied.

Education

It is also to be remembered that it is a very real economy in teaching power that each teacher shall have under her care a class and not an individual girl. The same time of preparation, and of class teaching, suffices for the class as well as for the individual; it is only in the correction of the pupils' work and in individual advice and counsel that the class is the more expensive both of time and strength. On the other hand, those of us who have taught a class are well aware of the more helpful inspiration and the more vivid interest bestowed by the class on its teacher, things which greatly compensate for the inevitable anxieties and increased toil.

Turning to a totally different view of the advantages of school over home education, it is really very remarkable to observe the unhoped-for improvement in health enjoyed by nearly all delicate children when their mothers are at last persuaded to send them quite away to boarding-school. There is no doubt that the regularity of school life, the suitability of the food provided, and the removal from the child of the dreadful feeling that she is the centre about which the whole home revolves, is an enormous relief to her. Some children enjoy being " fussed," others of a healthier moral constitution dislike it; but the fact of being " fussed," of being the centre of the universe,

43

is equally deleterious to both types of girls : the one is enervated, the other irritated.

Another class of frail barque that anxious mothers are unwilling to trust to the waves and currents of school life is the sensitive child. Undoubtedly there are certain natures which are too tremblingly alive to external influences, organisms whose nerves appear as if they lacked the ordinary protective covering; but for one child who is really unduly sensitive there are dozens whose supposed sensitiveness arises partly from bad temper and partly from an undue appreciation of their own importance. Children possess the vices and virtues of grown-up people in miniature, and the same qualities which make very difficult and anti-social units of some men and some women are to be found in boys and girls. The best antidote for a hot or sulky temper, and the best remedy for an over-valuation of self, is to be found in the mutual discipline exercised by children at school. The extra-sensitive child may find the first weeks, or even the first term, at school something of a change, and perhaps not altogether an acceptable change, from home life, but there are very few girls who do not rapidly adapt themselves to their circumstances, and therefore very few who do not soon enjoy the healthy atmosphere of their little republic.

Many mothers are unwilling to send their

Education

children to boarding-school, or indeed to school at all, for fear that their manners, morals, and religion may suffer. These mothers have heard evil reports of school-land, and not the most majestic bunches of the grapes of Eshcol as represented by scholarships and rewards will induce them to let their children go out to battle with the giants and ogres that they imagine as inhabiting the fruitful valleys and delectable mountains of the great world of school. To a large extent their anxieties are unfounded ; the moral and religious tone in most of the larger and better-known girls' schools is above reproach. The headmistress who sets a lofty example both to teachers and to girls will generally be rewarded by the existence in her school of what is known as a " good tone." It is true that from time to time an unfortunate, neglected, or depraved child may introduce moral infection, but such a serious accident is rare, and in a well-managed school the evil does not spread. The trouble is quickly recognised, and is dealt with without delay.

As a rule, the mental and moral atmosphere of school is really healthier for the young girl than is the atmosphere of home. The arrangements at school, the books to be found there, the style of conversation, and the interests of the little community are more suitable to the adolescent girl than are the more mixed interests, conversation, and literature to be found in her own home.

Adolescent girls are in an extraordinarily unstable and plastic condition, with opinions, tastes, and customs that are altering rapidly, even from day to day. It is better for them that, until their opinions, tastes, and habits have attained some degree of stability, their environment at any rate shall be stable. The only children who might with any colourable probability be thought to be better for home education are those children who are deficient either in mind or in body. Girls who are backward, and who at the age of 10 or 12 have only the capacity of children of 6 or 7, children who are the subjects of epileptic fits, or of serious brain storms leading to ungovernable attacks of passion, do need a special environment. But of a truth such children need not the isolation of home, but the discipline of a special community where they can receive skilled and sympathetic instruction and management. Schools for the deficient, the feeble-minded, and the epileptic are increasing in number amongst us; they are already available for the children of the poor, and to a certain extent, but unfortunately much less freely, they are available for the children of the professional and leisured classes. Demand is necessary to create supply, and parents have been reluctant and backward in seeking a special environment for those of their children who need it most. They do not consider that the afflicted child is grievously defrauded when it is brought up without discipline and without that amount of education which can be conferred by special teachers under special circumstances. Nor do they consider the injustice done to the other members of the household, and especially to the other children of the family, when the afflicted child, for whom special excuses and special arrangements have to be made, interferes at all turns with the normal life of the family.

Education has often been compared to a ladder rising gradually through the preparatory school, the public school, and college and university life to the great school of adult experience. Such a ladder should be available to every child of the nation, even though one substitutes for the former description of the ladder the terms elementary, secondary, and continuation schools and apprenticeship.

With regard to girls, it is a somewhat curious fact that several excellent colleges were started many years ago before the necessary development of high schools and public schools for girls had afforded a secure foundation for college and university education. Now, however, education for girls is becoming properly consolidated, and the rungs of the ladder follow each other in suitable gradation. Something remains to be done, and it is greatly to be hoped that the imprimatur of the university will be freely given not only to the girls who have studied arts, science, music, and medicine, but also to those whose aim in life is the higher kinds of secretarial and office work, and those who wish to make a special study of domestic economy, house, and mothercraft. The good days are evidently coming when young women will be as carefully trained for their primary and obvious calling of housewife and mother as they now are for the well-established professions of teacher, scientist, and doctor. The nation is slowly awakening to the fact that all honourable callings are to be honoured, and that all adequate and perfect service needs special and careful preparation.

There is little doubt that it is a great mistake for any girl to leave school while still in her teens and lapse into an objectless and therefore unhappy existence, waiting, like her ancestor of old in the slave market, for a suitable purchaser. It is pitiable that so many young lives should be virtually wasted because their development is cut short at so immature a stage.

Choice of a profession.—As with a religious vocation, so also is it with the ordinary vocations of life. The inward conviction of fitness must find its correlative in the suitability of outward circumstances. The desire of many girls to follow certain professions must be to some extent

Choice of a Profession

governed by the possibilities of their environment. Money, health of body, and mental
vigour must be adequate to secure probable
success. There is a distinct need that older and
more experienced people should make it their
duty and their pleasure to offer sympathetic
counsel to young women in these matters. To
some extent school teachers are able to discharge
this necessary function, but it is very desirable
that some of the senior members of each profession should make themselves available to
give this help. Take, for instance, the profession
of medicine. A girl's school teacher may know
whether she possesses a healthy body, a vigorous
mind, and a training that has qualified her for
the memorising of the many facts in anatomy,
physiology, chemistry, etc., and whether she has
also the judicial faculty that will enable her to
appreciate the symptoms and aspects of disease
and to keep all her work in proper perspective;
but she cannot know the length of time, the
amount of money, or the special gifts that are
needed for a really successful career as a doctor.
The girl who is likely to be useful and distinguished as a doctor needs all the qualifications that
would have fitted her for success in other professions, but she needs in addition other qualities,
such as knowledge of character, a great capacity
for loving sympathy, patience with the way-
ward and perverse, and an imagination which

will enable her to place herself in the position of her patients and to see their troubles from their point of view. The woman who cannot do this may be successful as a lecturer, she may even be a brilliant surgeon, but she could never be the wise counsellor of the sick and sorrowful, nor the efficient restorer of those whose sickness is as much of the heart and moral nature as of the physical frame.

To take another illustration. A girl may have decided talent for music or for art in one of its many branches, but it needs an expert in the profession of her choice to advise her whether she has sufficient physique and the necessary *moral* to stand without undue peril the difficult preparation that must be undergone. From what has been said it will be evident that in many instances a girl cannot choose entirely alone, and that even the help of her parents is not sufficient to enable her to decide aright unless one of them chances to belong to the profession which she wishes to follow.

Every girl should have a profession, and every girl should have the profession of her choice in view during the last few years of school life. It is, of course, quite possible that advancing years and increasing knowledge both of herself and of the world around her may lead to a change of opinion. The same thing happens with boys, but they are encouraged from very early years to think of their future, and, while avoiding all specialisation, to let their minds incline towards their choice.

The natural vocation for every woman is that of wife and mother, and in the training of every girl provision should be made for the acquisition of definite and accurate knowledge of the essentials of domestic economy and mothercraft. In the case of girls who have in their minds some other career, less knowledge of domestic economy and mothercraft may be demanded, but inasmuch as after some years spent in the chosen profession many girls marry, none can be entirely excused from this most essential branch of knowledge. The position of the young woman who marries without a knowledge of domestic affairs is really pitiable. If she has servants to superintend, they, and not she, are really in charge of the house, and when children come her helplessness and ineffectiveness are still more keenly felt. It has been noticed by those who have the duty of teaching women medical students that a young woman who has had some interval between her ordinary education and her medical studies makes the best student. A good many girls come to the medical school having spent some years as teachers, nurses, or scientists, and these young women are greatly assisted in their new work by their increased knowledge of the world, their

wider outlook, and their greater versatility.
Therefore, a few years given to the study of
domestic economy and cognate subjects is a
gain, and not a waste of time, even to the woman
who intends to make some totally different
profession her life-work.

Balance of activities. — No human being
ought to live a one-sided life. We are all
possessed of many faculties and many possibilities of self-development, and the happiest
and most efficient individuals are they whose
whole nature has been cultivated, and who have
many powers of usefulness and many sources
of enjoyment. The ideal woman is neither the
girl who spends her life in playing games, riding
horses, or training dogs, nor is she the girl who
spends her days in uninterrupted study, going
from lecture to lecture, working far into the hours
of the night, and eschewing the natural amusements and relaxations proper to her age and
to her station in life. One of the saddest parts
of the burden of the industrial classes under
present circumstances is the fact that nearly
all their waking life is spent in doing some one
thing; that they are bound to the wheel of
Fate, and have lost not only the opportunity, but
even the power to enjoy the wonderful things
by which they are surrounded. Even to these
workers some slight amelioration has come, and
more, we hope, will come; but in young people

Choice of a Profession

of the professional and leisured classes such a one-sided existence is unnecessary and wrong. There is no reason why college girls, music or art students, and embryo doctors should so overburden themselves with work preparatory to their profession as to have no leisure left for healthy exercise, and no opportunity for an occasional glimpse into a different and therefore an invigorating world. Incessant toil at any study tends to blunt the intellect and to take off the keen edge of enjoyment, and as a matter of fact the best work of which anyone is capable is only done while both body and mind are fresh enough for work to be a pleasure.

Once more, it is necessary to insist on the great value of Swedish exercises, games, and dances for the development and refreshment of the body, and on the value of swimming, bathing, and walking. One must also insist on the value of mental recreations, such as may be found in well-chosen books treating of subjects quite different from the chosen profession. To some an occasional concert, to others a really good play or opera, will cause the heart to sing with joy, while in addition to such relaxations time and money should always be found for a summer holiday, and this should be truly a holiday, a time in which professional studies are entirely laid aside, a time devoted to the beauties of Nature, to the wonders of art, to foreign travel, or, indeed, to anything that gives both mind and body entirely new interests and a fresh environment.

One word of caution may be useful in this connection. Young people are more adaptable than are their elders, and they do many things with impunity which would be disastrous at a later period of life; but even the young should not turn from eleven months of intellectual toil and comparative bodily inactivity to an over-strenuous walking tour or to the climbing of mountains, for the comfortable achievement of which muscles, heart, and lungs should have some adequate preparation. Here, again, we see how wise it is to maintain a daily balance of activities.

Moral education and sexual physiology. — By a natural transition we passed from the subject of education to that of the choice of a profession. We may now consider that branch of education which belongs more distinctively to the moral sphere, with special reference to sexual physiology.

Moral education should, of course, have begun long before the years of adolescence. In early childhood physical facts can be accepted by children without shock and without undue emphasis. Many parents shrink from imparting moral education, and more especially instruction in sexual physiology, to their children. Some of them think that it is wiser to do nothing in this direction; they believe that a child's mind is like a sheet of fair white paper, unwritten on and absolutely blank; they will not take the responsibility of writing on this virgin surface, they prefer to leave it to chance. Logically, they may fairly expect that the page will become dusty and flyblown, even if no worse defilement happens. As a matter of fact, the child's mind is not a fair, unwritten page; it is a *palimpsest;* and the writing on it achieved by the finger of heredity only awaits the interpretation of environment to show the good and the evil that have been already inscribed.

To lay aside a metaphor which must not be pressed too closely, the child's mind much more resembles the sensitised surface used in photography, and the picture to be developed thereon depends not only on the light of Heaven which shines on all alike, but on the influences which are permitted by the parent to make the record. To each parent is committed the awful responsibility, " Take this child and nurse it for me." The child is given to the parent, influenced already no doubt by heredity, but also subject to the influences that the environment of the parent must provide. In each father's and in each mother's ear the inexorable voice continues, " I will give thee thy wages "—the wages of success or failure of the child's life, the wages of comfort or of misery for those responsible for its failure or success. The responsibility cannot be escaped; it may be shirked, but the child is there, burdened or blessed with the heredity it has received, and open to the influences provided for it.

In the moral and sexual education of children one great principle must be observed : the truth, and nothing but the truth, is safe. Among the earliest problems of childhood are those great questions of " Whence came I ? " " What am I ? " These questions are forced on the child by the circumstances of life. The advent of the new baby, the arrival of the kittens and puppies, the eggs and the nestlings, are constantly before its eyes. Whence came those new and delightful beings ? Woe be to the parent who prevaricates, or, worse still, who lies. The punishment is immediate, and well fitted to the crime. In the futile endeavour to substitute ignorance for innocence the mother has slain her child's trust in her truth, and has to that extent at least injured its moral nature and handicapped its future. The mother need not fear that in telling her child the simple truth she will sully its purity. Little children read the tremendous facts recorded in the Gospels without question and without bewilderment. And so with domestic events. If the mother simply says, " It is God's good gift to us that we should have children, the cat kittens, and the dog puppies," she will be believed, and the child will make no undesirable application of the knowledge. After a time further questions may still be met truthfully. The child will see for itself that there is a relation between the mother and the offspring, and this natural relation can be explained, beautified, and sanctified by telling the eager little listener how God provides the sanctuary of the mother's body, just as He provides the protection of the eggshell for the tiny feeble life which would perish if exposed to the cold and the violence of the world. The child will feel an added tenderness and devotion to the mother who thus warmed, nourished, and protected its early days, and the girl more especially will look forward to the time when the motherly yearnings which are a part of her nature shall find their natural fulfilment.

A little later on the father's part in the beginning of life may be reverently and beautifully taught through lessons in vegetable physiology. The fertilising *pollen* or cells from the *anther* may be studied under the microscope, and similarly their scattering on the female part of the flower, the *stigma*, can be seen, and with a microscope or strong lens the pollen tubes may be seen conveying the vital principle from the stigma down into the *ovary*. Here in the ovary may be demonstrated the female contribution or *ovules*, carefully packed together, beautifully arranged, each awaiting fertilisation. The fertilised ovule, when matured, is set free from the receptacle, and falls to the ground, and in due course the new plant germinates, its root strikes downwards, its stem grows upwards, and with the development of leaf, of flower, and of its essential organs the wonderful cycle is complete.

All this knowledge can be most reverently and beautifully conveyed. Nothing is more interesting or delightful to a child than such fairy stories, beautiful stories which have the merit of truth as well as the glamour of wonder.

The child who has thus been taught the fundamental facts of creaturely existence will gladly accept the further teaching that all life is of God, that we came from God, that we live in God, and that we go to God—that in Him we live and move and have our being. The child learns that we owe everything to God, and that as He has bestowed the great gift of procreation on men and women, the human body is not only physically beautiful, artistically wonderful, but is also absolutely sacred. It must be taught that the body is a sacred trust, that it is to be developed to the best of our powers, that it is to be defended from all injury and from all dishonour, that anything that makes the body weak, or sick, or degraded is a grievous sin both against the body and against its Creator. After a time, when the child goes to school and mixes with others less carefully nurtured, it will be necessary to say that the functions of the body are holy and good in themselves, but that they may be wrongly used, and that if wrongly used sorrow and disease are likely to follow.

One further caution should be given. The functions of the body are sacred in themselves and should also be sacred as matters of conversation; they are not to be talked about or discussed; they are fitting subjects for prayer and for the intimate confidences between parent and child, but they are not to be discussed with other people, for " a stranger doth not intermeddle with his joy."

PART II

THE YOUNG WIFE

CHAPTER I

PREPARATION FOR MARRIAGE

A WOMAN's preparation for marriage may be considered under two heads : (1) General; (2) Special.

1. The **general** preparation of a girl for marriage ought to begin with her life. The question whether she is to be a really good wife and mother depends largely on the nature and nurture that her own parents give her. As will have appeared from the earlier pages of this book, there is no limit to the care, the intelligence, and the devotion that ought to be lavished upon each young girl.

We have already seen that the fate of every human being is largely influenced by two great factors, heredity and environment. If the young wife is the healthy child of healthy parents, and has inherited from them soundness of her whole nature, and if in addition to this the circumstances of her life have been such as to strengthen the good and to repress the evil, her chances of health, happiness, and efficiency as a wife are enormously increased.

One of the great duties of a wife is to be a wise and sympathetic companion to her husband ; it is well for them both when the wife possesses a good general education and has also tastes and aims in life either similar or complementary to those of her husband. Exact similarity of character and temperament is both unattainable and unnecessary. Frequently the happiest marriages, like the happiest friendships, are found where the gifts and ambitions of the partners are widely dissimilar, but if so they must at least be complementary to each other. With regard to this aspect of matrimony, the foundation of a thoroughly good general education, together with readiness of insight and quickness of sympathy, is essential. A woman before marriage may have had no special knowledge, let us say, of music, painting, or literature, but when she marries a musician, a painter, or an author she ought to be fitted by her general education, and by her readiness of perception and sympathy, to take an intelligent interest in her husband's work, even if, owing to dissimilarity of taste and training, she is not fitted to be his collaborator.

A woman's second qualification for a happy marriage is her ability to make the best of her husband's circumstances and to secure for him and for her family the maximum amount of good and advantage from the means at her disposal. This is equally true whether the husband be a king or a labourer. The principle is exactly the same : the wife's duty and pleasure lie in adapting the means to the end, and, whether her duties are those of a queen or those of the humblest housewife, she should be able to use all that comes into her hands for the best advantage of the husband and children who are dependent on her for their ability to live the life that is ideal for each family in its own sphere.

The third and the greatest duty of a wife is that she should be " a joyful mother of children." Thoughtful people have always recognised that on the fertility of a nation obviously depends its power to fill its territories, to colonise, and to extend its power. Less obviously, but equally truly, on the fertility of a nation depends its ability to raise up men and women of light and leading to guide, instruct, and defend the nation as a whole. Men and women of distinction may be looked on as the fine flowers of a nation, and they are likely to be produced in greater abundance when the vitality, the fertility of the nation is at its maximum. It is not more than fifty years ago since the populations of France and Germany were approximately equal, but, owing apparently to habits of luxury, self-indulgence, and perhaps selfishness, the birth-rate of

France has gradually fallen until the population has become stationary at about thirty-eight millions. On the other hand, Germany, which fifty years ago possessed a much simpler civilisation, and was beginning to be possessed by a desire for expansion, for colonisation, and for world empire, continues to have a relatively high (though rapidly falling) birth-rate, so that at the present time the population is about sixty-eight millions. The power of a nation, both in peace and in war, depends very largely on the size of its population, and so long as large tracts of the earth's surface remain sparsely populated, there is no reason why the fall of the birth-rate should be viewed with contentment.

Many causes may be assigned for the fall of the birth-rate which obtains more or less in all civilised countries, and, indeed, it appears to fall more or less strictly in proportion to the artificiality of each country's civilisation. In accordance with this we are prepared to find that France led the way, and that Britain was not slow to follow, and, further, that of late years the influence has reached Germany; while the birth-rate in countries less artificial, which retain much of the primitive instincts of mankind — such, for instance, as Russia — has not as yet been affected. The increasing complexity of civilisation, together with mounting wealth and a growing desire for a more comfortable or a more luxurious standard of living, has led to the limitation of families. Even in our own land we find that whereas the uneducated and thriftless continue to have relatively large families — an average of something over seven children being born to each couple—ordinarily well-to-do people have an average of somewhere about three children to a family, whilst amongst the most highly educated and wealthiest families in the community there are but 1·5 children to each union. A sad commentary on this racial suicide has been afforded during the War, for in the newspaper notices recording the names of those who have fallen we all too frequently find the phrases " only son " or " only child."

In considering this subject it is necessary to remember that in many instances the absence, or the strict limitation, of families is the result of an honest, although we believe a mistaken, wish to do the best either for the couple themselves or for the one or two children of the union. A husband and wife whose own education has been curtailed, and whose position in life has been injured by the insufficient means of their own parents, are very likely to suppose that on their own limited income they are unable to do justice to the needs of children. Such honest but mistaken couples do not take into consideration the fact that, inasmuch as they owe their own lives to their country, so the least that they can do in return is to furnish her with children who will be prepared to take their place later on. Still less do they reflect that, inasmuch as some men and women never marry and some married couples are inevitably childless, the birth of two children to a fertile union does not suffice. This insufficiency is still further emphasised by the number of children and young people who die before they themselves have had any chance of adding to the number of the nation. Probably, taking all factors into consideration, each fertile married couple should hope to have five or six children.

The moral and religious aspect of the subject may not appeal, as does the national, to everyone, but it cannot be overlooked. The churches —Jewish, Roman, and Anglican—have always held that, inasmuch as the main object of matrimony is the procreation of children, it is a wrong, and a sin against matrimony and its Divine Author, that there should be any interference with natural fertility.

Lastly, from the point of view of health, the strict limitation of family that has become general is deleterious to the health of the wife. Several witnesses who appeared before the Birth-rate Commission, 1918–15, gave evidence to the effect that even where no physical injury was produced by contra-conceptive devices, nervous troubles were more frequent in women who had refused or who had been prevented from having a normal number of children.

2. With regard to the **special** preparation for marriage, the mother or other nearest female relation should satisfy herself that the prospective bride is in a satisfactory condition of health, and that she is physically fit for the duties that she will be called on to perform. It is nothing short of cruel to allow a young couple to enter on the momentous obligations of married life without both parties to that union being carefully examined by a trustworthy medical adviser, and mutually receiving the assurance that they are in good health, and not only in good general health, but that they are fit for their new and onerous duties. Formerly it would have been thought indelicate and most extraordinary if a girl had gone of her own accord to a doctor with a request for a general examination and for a special assurance of fitness. This request is, however, becoming fairly frequent, and women doctors are often asked to certify not only to the condition of the lungs, the heart, and digestive apparatus, but also as to whether the organs of generation are normal and whether they may be expected to fulfil their allotted functions. Formerly it was by no means uncommon for unfortunate brides to say that they had been shocked by learning *after marriage* the facts of married life that they ought to have known before mar-

riage. Weird stories were told of women who had gone through the ceremony of marriage and who, after months had passed, were still wives only in name, because they had been unable to understand, or to consent to, their husbands' lawful demands. It is quite possible—nay, it is even desirable—that young girls should learn much physiology, and even the physiology of the reproductive organs, without in any way understanding how such knowledge may personally apply to themselves ; but the personal application of knowledge which is most undesirable for the adolescent is an absolute necessity for the prospective bride. No girl ought to be permitted to promise to undertake duties which she does not understand ; it is a very bad foundation for married happiness. Therefore, the girl's mother, if able and willing to give the knowledge, should do so, and if she be not, the young bride should be instructed kindly and sympathetically by a doctor, preferably by one of her own sex.

Somewhat akin to this knowledge of the structure and functions of her own body is the advice that ought to be given to young women as to their choice of a husband. Love may be blind, but marriage may open the eyes in an undesirable fashion, and no man and no woman should permit themselves to enter into a contract for life without being satisfied, either through personal knowledge or through the knowledge of their parents, that the proposed partner is in all respects suitable. Some knowledge of the prospective husband's social and financial position has always been customary, and in many instances the father of the bride has been expected to state what he can do for his daughter in the present and in the future. But with regard to the all-important question of health and of moral standing, no such inquiries have been made. On the contrary, so far as the man is concerned, it has been customary to ask nothing, and apparently to care little, as to the past. The bride's character and reputation have always been expected to be above reproach—an unfair and an unwise discrimination ; but in the tremendous matter of health nothing has been required of either husband or wife. Parents who would not permit their daughter to marry a poor man, and who, very properly, would not permit her union with an unemployed or commercially dishonourable man, have cheerfully contemplated her marriage with a man suffering himself from disease, or in whose family tubercle, alcohol, or other racial poisons may have been dominant. In this way the most grievous injustice has been done ; pure, innocent, and healthy girls have been married to men who could never be satisfactory to them as husbands or as fathers of their children. Grievous injustice has also been done to the nation, for lunacy, tuberculosis, syphilis, and other sources of weakness and inefficiency have been thus propagated.

A Royal Commission for the investigation of Venereal Diseases sat from 1918 to 1915. It received an enormous amount of evidence as to the nature of these scourges, and an especially interesting portion of it showed not only how syphilis has the power of causing misery and possibly early death in the man who contracts it, but also how very probable it is that he will infect his wife. In such cases pregnancy may end in miscarriage, in premature still-birth, or in the birth of children who survive for a short period only, and who, should they unfortunately outlive infancy, swell the returns of our blind asylums, deaf asylums, hospitals for the insane, and prisons. It is quite true that in past years the injustice to the young people themselves and to the nation was little known and still less appreciated; therefore, it is possible to condone, if not to pardon, the carelessness and ineptitude of the past; but in the face of such facts as have been published and commented on in connection with this Royal Commission, there is now no excuse for the marriage of the sick with the healthy, and no reason why there should not be a careful investigation as to the fitness of couples for the production of healthy children for the service of the State.

CHAPTER II

THE DIFFICULTIES OF EARLY MARRIED LIFE

THE difficulties of early married life may arise from many causes. To begin with, married life is altogether different from life during courtship. The husband and wife necessarily see much more of each other, and they see each other with changed eyes. Before marriage, romance, glamour, and high expectation combine together to assist in a process of idealisation, but after marriage the very intimacy which had been pictured as so delightful, and which, indeed, ought to be so delightful, compels the recognition that, after all, the beloved partner is human, not divine. The more closely people live together, the narrower the space of the home, the less the chances of outside interest and the smaller the financial margin, the more rapidly do husband and wife find the necessity for mutual forbearance and for patience. The delightful fallacy that money insufficient for one would be practically wealth for two is soon exposed, and happy are the young people who have enough common sense, mutual love, and respect to sit down to their bread and butter and be content with the absence of ambrosia. Much happiness was expected by both, and much happiness both will have, upon condition that both can be satisfied with the reasonable and the possible, and that they are no longer babies disposed to cry for the unattainable.

Household difficulties.—Real married life, the management of an ordinary household, is very different from the doll-housekeeping of childish days. In the doll's house the actors of the little drama were all entirely subservient to the will of the over-lord; the cooks did not spoil the dinner, the parlourmaids did not break the plates, no one destroyed one's dearest treasures, and the voice of impatience and of quarrel was never heard. But in one's own home, disappointment and worries are all too prone to enter; the shortcomings of servants, the apparently unreasonable demands of one's husband, and one's own still more unreasonable deficiencies, falterings, and failures of temper lead to much searching of heart. In some such cases the young woman feels by no means sure that it was well to marry; she may even look back regretfully to the days when she was a "bachelor-girl" with no one to please but herself. The wise woman will take to herself a robust and healthy optimism; she will refuse to be depressed by the natural human failings whether of her servants, her husband, or herself. It is true that "a man's foes shall be they of his own household," and even more true that one's worst foe is one's self. Let the battle be once won against that arch enemy, let selfishness be slain, and let the young wife resolutely determine to play her part, to be true to herself, to be patient with all, including even herself, and one can safely promise her that she will be "happy though married."

The young wife will also do well to bear in mind that her foes, like one's political enemies, are apt to rush up fresh attacks where they were least expected, that they will fall upon her weakest spot, and may gain a partial, fleeting victory before she can make the counter-attack. However, as we have learnt by much experience in the field, the taking of a trench or two makes no difference to the ultimate end of the campaign. The young wife must dig herself in with patience, she must send her scouts aloft to afford her timely notice of the next attack, and she must be ready with other weapons than shot and shell to face the slings and arrows of outrageous fortune. She may take heart of grace, for after a time she will learn that mixture of firmness and suavity that is necessary to the management of her fellow-creatures; she will also, after a time, acquire that blessed elasticity which will enable her to take with smiling equanimity the querulous remarks of an over-

Difficulties of Early Married Life

tired and very worried man, who also himself has his daily battlefield and who looks for the support and co-operation of a cheerful ally when he comes home from his dubious contest.

And so the first difficult days of married life may be well spent. The young housewife will daily advance in the difficult task of making the most of a slender income. The money that in the early days seemed as if it would not suffice for bread and meat is gradually so well managed, and the cooking is so greatly improved, that good digestion, cheerfulness, and even some small luxuries can be compassed with the same outlay.

Advent of children.—After a few months, if both husband and wife are in good health and if the powers of Nature have had fair play, there may be reason to hope for the blessing of a family, and with this hope there comes a new interest in life. It is very important that, as explained a few pages back, both husband and wife should understand that it is really a privilege as well as a duty to fulfil the natural obligations of the married state. Nothing should be done by either husband or wife to prevent conception. Not infrequently a young couple agree that they will postpone the commencement of a family until, in their opinion, their financial position or other circumstances make it convenient. Unfortunately, in many instances the postponed child never arrives. When, after some few years of marriage, the couple conclude that they are ready and willing to accept the offered blessing, they find to their disappointment and sorrow that the wife is no longer apt for conception. It is difficult to explain exactly why such disabilities should arise. It is quite possible that the preventive measures taken were such as did not appear to entail any injury to the wife; all the same, she may be found to be suffering from congestion of the internal generative organs, or, even without any evident disease or trouble, her health is less good than it should be, and in spite of an honest although belated effort to carry out the duties of the married state, no results follow. Probably there is some subtle nervous injury which cannot be seen by the doctor and is only vaguely felt by the patient, but the fact remains that in many instances the desire for children which arises some years after marriage is never gratified.

In the evidence offered to the Birth-rate Commission several specialists, as mentioned in the preceding chapter, agreed that women who had few or no children were more liable to become nervous and invalidish. By no witness was any specific injury alleged; it appeared to them to be simply that, as is the case in other natural instincts, either the desire or the power to carry it into effect depends on its proper and timely gratification. In giving this testimony the witnesses

Difficulties of Early Married Life

most carefully safeguarded themselves against being supposed to mean that sexual desire should be gratified apart from matrimony. The idea that virility and fertility depend in any way on the gratification of desire apart from marriage, and that a man's health suffers in consequence of abstention from premarital sexual intercourse, was denied by everyone; and probably there is not at the present time any doctor of modern education and good repute who would give the immoral and dangerous advice that was not uncommonly given some years ago. Doctors now know quite well, and are anxious to instruct the public, that, apart from marriage with its natural intimacy and lawful desire, a man's health and virility are in no danger from continence. The witnesses were also careful to emphasise the fact that gratification of desire apart from marriage is only too likely to lead to the contraction of disease which has far-reaching and disastrous effects. Doctors are anxious for the public to understand that, so far as scientific knowledge goes, evil is wrought not by continence but by improper indulgence. It may be conceded that a man's passions are stronger than a woman's, but it is an open question whether this additional strength of passion is not the result of education. Girls are taught from childhood that any exhibition of sexual feeling is unwomanly and intolerable; they also learn from an early age that if a woman makes a mistake it is upon her and upon her alone that social punishment will descend; consequently for generations, ever since the civilisation of society, women have perforce been habitually continent, and more than continent—modest and discreet.

Society has condoned incontinence in men, but has visited incontinence in women with severe condemnation. The time, however, has now come in which a higher morality and a better instructed regard for the true interests of the race have led to the demand that a man's life should be under as strict discipline as is that of a woman. If this demand is to be made and carried into effect, mothers will have to begin to teach their little boys self-control just in the same way as they have always taught it to their little girls. Not only must impurity and absolute wrongdoing be checked, but the lesson of self-control and self-reverence must be taught to all children alike.

One cannot but sympathise with the natural and proper desire of each couple to ensure that they shall have sufficient means to maintain and to educate their family. It is impossible in the present state of society to arrange in the mass that every child shall have equal opportunities; but it is quite possible to arrange that any individual child shall have the best possible education. The State provides elementary education which, although far from perfect, at any rate gives the chance that its recipients shall have a good groundwork of elementary knowledge, and from this platform there are many ladders by which the higher planes of secondary and even university education may be attained. Probably in the near future additional facilities will be provided, and it is to be hoped that before long the national conscience may be so awakened that, instead of parents thwarting the efforts of the educational authorities, they will gladly co-operate with them, and do their best to secure for their children the advantages which up to the present time have been too frequently neglected. No doubt it is difficult for the poorer parents of the community to realise the importance to their children of adequate food, sufficiency of fresh air and of rest and sleep, yet all these things are necessary in order that the children shall be capable of benefiting by the education which the ratepayers provide for them. The children's future must not be sacrificed for the sake of the few shillings they can earn weekly by working before and after school hours.

Physical difficulties.—In other cases the difficulties of early married life depend on the health of the husband or wife, or on some physical peculiarity. It is not at all infrequent for a

young couple to find that, with the heartiest
desire to fulfil the duties of the married state,
and with the greatest love for each other, there
is some physical impediment to the consummation of marriage. The most frequent of these
difficulties is constituted by a closure more or
less complete of the female passage, the *vagina*.
In virgins the vagina is partly closed by a membrane called the *hymen*. The space that is left
suffices amply for the passage of the menstrual
fluid, and as a rule after marriage the rupture
of this hymen makes the act of marriage possible,
and even easy. If, however, the membrane is
unusually thick and firm, or if it be unusually
parchment-like and tough, the husband's efforts
may fail to break it down, and then a painful
state of affairs commences ; there is a good
deal of nervous and moral distress, the husband
fears to hurt his wife by persistence, and the
wife, although she may brace up her courage
and endeavour to endure, in some instances
finds that this is impossible. Should the couple
then persist in their attempts, considerable
inflammation and swelling of the woman's external organs result. Not infrequently neither
husband nor wife likes to seek advice for this
condition. Their efforts may be persistent and
lead to increased physical distress, or they may
give up the attempt, believing it to be hopeless,
and then a still greater moral and mental dis-

Difficulties of Early Married Life

tress results. The wife feels that she is unsatisfactory, and is tempted to wish that she had never married ; or the husband may believe that it is his fault, and brood over his supposed impotence until perhaps he thinks that it is irremediable, and with his courage and his cheerfulness there goes to some extent his physical ability. In a more extreme case it is sometimes (but very rarely) found that there is an absolute impotence on the part of either husband or wife. In the case of the wife the natural formation of the parts may be such as actually to prohibit the physical side of marriage ; while the husband, from ill health or other original peculiarity, is in a still lesser number of cases really impotent.

It is very desirable that before marriage the bride and bridegroom should be carefully examined, as suggested in the previous chapter, not only with regard to their freedom from disease, but also with a view to determining whether each party is apt for matrimony. In the great majority of cases both husband and wife are perfectly fitted for matrimony; in the small minority of cases in which there is any unfitness the condition generally admits of remedy. For instance, should it be a case of an unduly thick hymen or insufficient hymeneal orifice, a removal of the redundant hymen or a dilatation of the orifice will make matrimony normal.

The Seven Ages of Woman

The third class of difficulties of early married life arises where there is disease in either partner. It would tend to the present comfort, and still more to the future welfare of young couples, if any deviation from perfect health were attended to immediately. More especially should advice be sought in cases where the consummation of marriage is followed by redness, swelling, pain, and discharge. Neither husband nor wife can in any case judge whether these symptoms are likely to be transient and need only the simplest remedies, or are of serious importance and only to be cured by careful and expert treatment.

CHAPTER III

PREGNANCY

THE origin of life depends on the ripening of an egg, and this egg is almost invariably due to the successful union of two elements—a sperm cell derived from the male and a germ cell derived from the female parent. This process may be seen in plants, sometimes with the naked eye, as in the case of the lily, and sometimes only by means of the microscope. In the vegetable world and in the lower members of the animal world we are not able to discern that consciousness accompanies conjugation, and in the case of fishes it happens that the female lays her eggs and swims away before the male comes and deposits his fertilising cells. But from the order of fishes upwards to man the conjunction of the sexes appears to be voluntary, to be inspired by mutual admiration and love, and usually to be accompanied by pleasure.

In the higher orders of animals and in the human being the eggs of the female are matured in the *ovaries*, internal glands situated in the pelvis, one on each side of the uterus. In the human female one or more of these eggs matures every month and is conveyed through the oviduct into the uterus. Either in the uterus or before its arrival at its destination, the ovum, or germ cell, may meet with the spermatozoon or fertilising cell derived from the male. Each spermatozoon is a cell furnished with a long hair-like appendage called a tail. When the head of the spermatozoon penetrates the germ cell of the ovum the tail breaks off and is left behind. Wonderful changes immediately occur within the ovum. Further details of this most interesting process may be learned from elementary books on physiology. The fertilised ovum sinks into the depths of the mucous membrane covering the inside of the womb, and the process known as *conception* is then complete.

The development of the pregnant uterus is one of the most surprising facts in Nature. In nine months it grows from a small body, the size of a jargonelle pear, having an inside measurement of about one and a half inches, a superficies of about twelve square inches, and weighing approximately one ounce, to be an organ large enough to accommodate a full-grown baby with the fluid in which it floats, and its organ of nutrition, called the *placenta*. The cavity of the uterus at full term is about 12 inches in length, the superficies of the organ contains some 520 square inches, and its weight (without the child and other contents) is a pound or more.

Pregnancy

At first the connection of the embryo with the wall of the womb is slender and easily broken down; it consists of minute branching processes called *villi*, which penetrate into the thickened, softened mucous membrane, and draw from it the nourishment on which the progressive growth and development of the embryo depend. From the end of the third month the union between the wall of the womb and the child's portion of what is known as the placenta becomes increasingly firm and intricate, the villi branch in every direction, and the mucous membrane becomes enormously developed and hypertrophied. At the end of pregnancy the placenta has the appearance of a disc-like cake, reddish-grey in colour, having a diameter of from 8 to 10 inches and a thickness at or about the centre of $1\frac{1}{4}$ inches. At the thickest point originates the *funis* or *navel cord*, which consists of blood-vessels embedded in a mass of tough jelly, whereby the nutrient material in the mother's blood is conveyed to the growing child. Not only is nutriment conveyed but the child's blood is oxygenated and purified in the placenta by interchange of its gases with the relatively pure gases of the mother's circulation.

The embryo grows from the microscopic speck of jelly that represents the united male and female cells until it becomes the creature of delightful colouring, beautiful curves, and active movement that we see after its birth. The changes are, of course, very gradual, and at first it needs the assistance of a lens and an expert eye to trace the constant development; but from the third month onwards anyone can recognise that the constantly growing embryo is truly a miniature human being, gradually attaining its appointed development. The fragile creature is protected from shocks by a thin, transparent, but tough membrane, the *amnion*, enclosed in which is a watery fluid known as the *liquor amnii*.

It is easy to understand that so great and wonderful a development occurring within her body must make a great difference to the functions and appearance of its mother. As a rule, a healthy woman remains in good health throughout pregnancy; some minor inconveniences she must suffer, but where all the successive changes are physiological, and where the woman herself remains in good health, there is nothing in the state of pregnancy to be characterised as abnormal, and still less as a state of illness.

The **signs and symptoms of pregnancy** fall quite naturally for description into three periods : (1) The first three months, up to the end of the development of the placenta. (2) The second period, up to the end of the twenty-eighth week, when the child is supposed to be able to maintain an independent existence. (8) To the end of full term —i.e. the end of the fortieth week.

Pregnancy

Cessation of menstruation. — The first symptom to attract the mother's attention is usually the absence of one or more periods. The majority of women are so far regular that the entire omission of one period of menstruation would attract their attention and suggest to them that pregnancy had commenced. Unluckily this phenomenon cannot be regarded as a *certain* sign, because it occasionally happens that the periods may cease owing to ill-health, especially owing to anæmia, commencing consumption, and mental disorders. On the other hand, pregnancy may have commenced and yet the periods may persist for at any rate three months, and in some cases a flow of blood, indistinguishable from menstruation, may continue even up to term. Still, the rule holds good that the first noticeable symptom of pregnancy is the cessation of the period.

Mammary development. — Very shortly after the beginning of pregnancy — say from six to eight weeks—the patient experiences sensations of fullness, tenderness, and pricking of the breasts. On examination it is seen that these organs have increased in size, that the veins in the skin covering them are bluer and more obvious than in the non-pregnant condition. The coloured part around the nipple called the *areola* becomes deeper in colour and slightly puffy in appearance. The deepening of colour continues throughout pregnancy ; in the fair woman the delicate shell-like pink becomes a deeper rose colour, and finally somewhat brownish-red ; in the case of brunettes the areola becomes a pinkish-brown, gradually deepening in colour until it is very dark brown, almost black. In both types of women there soon develops a quantity of small spot-like organs known as Montgomery's follicles, and from about the fourth month the ordinary areola is surrounded by a more faintly tinted zone, the colour of which looks as if it had been discharged here and there by drops of water. This zone is known as the secondary areola.

Morning sickness.—Nearly all women suffer more or less from nausea or vomiting in the early months of pregnancy, and although this disagreeable phenomenon goes by the name of morning sickness, because it is usually most marked when the woman rises from bed, yet it may sometimes, even in cases of perfect health, recur at intervals during the day. In some respects it resembles sea-sickness ; it usually comes on quite suddenly, without any obvious cause, and culminates in a free evacuation of the contents of the stomach, after which the patient feels comfortable. Unfortunately, the comfort is not always of long duration. The patient must not worry herself and think that she is ill because she is sick; it is quite natural; indeed, some people go so far as to think that it is beneficial. Morning sickness may start very early in pregnancy and continue even to the end, but in the great majority of cases it begins between the sixth and eighth weeks and subsides shortly after the end of the third month.

SECOND PERIOD

Increase in size of the uterus and abdomen.—In the very beginning of pregnancy no increase of size can be noted, for the womb is at that time contained within the bony circle of the pelvis, and its enlargement is so slight as not to be perceptible. Shortly after the end of the third month the top of the uterus lies a little higher than the pubic bone, and therefore may be felt in thin women, especially when they have soft and lax abdominal walls, but it is not likely that any woman would be able to notice so small an enlargement herself unless these conditions of the abdominal wall were present. From this time onwards the uterus with its contents grows rapidly, and certainly from the fifth month the patient can readily notice that there is a central globular mass, and that its size increases week by week.

Quickening.—Somewhere between the sixteenth and twentieth week of pregnancy the woman is able to appreciate that she has something alive and capable of movement within her. No doubt movements of the embryo commence much earlier, but they are feeble and not easily noticed. At first the sensation is slight and vague, and has been compared by some patients to the movements of a bird held in the two hands. Shortly, however, very definite movements of the limbs can be recognised, and indeed may become much too definite for comfort. It is well for the expectant mother to know that she ought to feel the movements of her child, for she will then not be alarmed or disconcerted, but will be thankful for the evidence that her child is alive and increasing in strength.

Sounds of the foetal heart.—From about the same time as that at which quickening occurs the sounds of the baby's heart can be heard by an ear placed on the lower part of the abdomen immediately above the right or the left groin. Of course, the patient herself cannot hear this, but it can be heard by any observant and intelligent person. The sound of the foetal heart greatly resembles that of a watch ticking under a pillow. The rate of the pulsation depends on the size and development of the child. While it is still small the beats may be as many as 160 to the minute ; but as time goes on and the foetus increases in weight and vigour the rate diminishes, until just before birth it is usually somewhere about 140 to the minute.

Pregnancy

There are other signs connected with this second period of pregnancy, but inasmuch as they can only be appreciated by the medical attendant it is useless to describe them in such a work as this.

THIRD PERIOD

Secretion of milk.—During the last twelve weeks of pregnancy the mother will notice an intensification of all the symptoms already described. The breasts will be more developed in all respects, and now the presence of milk will be readily detected. Milk is secreted from a very early period of pregnancy, and may sometimes be noticed even by the mother as early as the third month ; but it becomes more evident and more abundant as pregnancy progresses, and towards the end it may even flow with or without gentle pressure on the breast.

Alterations in the umbilicus.—During the early weeks of pregnancy the umbilicus is probably a little deeper than in the non-pregnant state ; gradually, however, as the abdominal wall grows and stretches, the umbilicus becomes shallower. It is approximately level with the abdominal wall about the twenty-eighth week, and becomes more and more raised above the surface and prominent up to full term.

Pigmentary changes.—The pigmentation of the areola of the breast and also of the mid-line of the abdomen leading from the umbilicus to the pubes becomes somewhat obvious as pregnancy proceeds, and is always better marked in brunettes. It is, however, not limited to these parts of the body. There is a tendency to a deepening of colour all over the skin, and more especially in such parts as the armpits, folds of the elbows and knees, and in the groins. The pigmentation is generally diffuse, but may occasionally be circumscribed here and there so as rather to resemble a smudge of dirt. It is of no importance whatever, but it is well to recognise that it frequently occurs in order that no alarm may be felt when it is discovered.

Subsidence of the abdomen. — Some time before birth, at a period varying from a few days to a month or more, a very remarkable change occurs in the condition of the abdomen. As a rule, about the thirty-fifth or thirty-sixth week the rounded upper margin of the uterus can be felt at a level with the lower ribs, completely filling the available space and sometimes stretching the abdominal wall. The presenting part of the child, usually the head, is driven into the cavity of the pelvis by the painless contractions of the womb, which become stronger as pregnancy advances, and about the end of the eighth month it is so far driven in that the upper margin descends appreciably, leaving the upper part of the abdomen freer and more available for the accommodation of the bowels. As a result of this the pressure is lessened on the mother's heart and lungs, and therefore she feels able to breathe and to digest in greater comfort. On the other hand, the presence of the lower portion of the womb containing the presenting part of the child necessarily exercises greater pressure on the bladder and on the lower bowel. In consequence of this the patient may suffer from constipation or from a disagreeable sense of irritability of the bowel, and also from an increased frequency of micturition. The patient ought to welcome these changes, because they show that the baby is not too large in proportion to the size of her bony pelvis, and therefore it is a guarantee that there will be no severe mechanical hindrance to the process of childbirth.

Duration of pregnancy. — Every woman who believes herself to be pregnant is anxious to know how she shall calculate, and frequently much inconvenience is caused by miscalculation. The general rule is that labour should be expected at what would otherwise be the beginning of the tenth monthly period. This can be readily ascertained by marking off in a calendar forty weeks from the commencement of the last period. But as calendars are not always available, it is customary to calculate nine calendar months from seven days after the commencement of the last period, adding two or three days to this calculation if February is included among the months reckoned. Thus, a woman whose period began on March 1st would reckon to December 8th, whereas if her period commenced on December 1st she would expect about September 10th, because February has to be included.

In spite of all good and careful calculations, it not infrequently happens that a baby arrives before or after its expected date, and yet there is nothing about the child to indicate prematurity or post-maturity. There are several sources of error. Thus, instead of a woman conceiving immediately after the end of her period she may have conceived immediately before the next expected period, which would introduce an error of about three weeks. On the other hand, it may happen that one or even more periods may appear after pregnancy has commenced, and that therefore a fully matured child may be born at what the mother calculates to be the termination of the seventh, eighth, or ninth month. It is therefore necessary in all cases to correct the original calculation. The doctor does this partly by observing the rate of growth of the womb and contained child. The upper margin of the uterus is supposed to be on a level with the umbilicus at the sixth month, and quickening is supposed to occur approximately at the mid-term of pregnancy; therefore when the movements of

Pregnancy

the child are noticed it is fair to conclude that at any rate another twenty weeks of pregnancy remain to be fulfilled. It must be confessed, however, that with all care, and with all available corrections, it is very difficult to be accurate. Dr. Matthews Duncan with Scotch caution suggested that the expected date of delivery should be regarded as the middle day of a fortnight within which parturition might be expected.

CHAPTER IV

DOMESTIC MANAGEMENT OF PREGNANCY

FAR more important than the calculation of the duration of pregnancy is its careful and successful management; on this depends the welfare of both mother and child. The rules given for the management of a young girl's health apply also to the health of the young mother, but they need to be more intelligently pursued and more strictly enforced than is customary. It is a great mistake to suppose that ordinary healthy pregnancy partakes in any way of the nature of ill-health. The process is a natural one, and ought to call forth the best powers with which the expectant mother is endowed. It is, however, to be remembered that, although pregnancy is normal, it is a condition of considerable stress, and that the organs of the mother's body are working harder than they ever worked before. She is now called upon to provide not only for the nourishment of her own body but for that of the constantly growing child, which makes increasing demands on her powers. Her heart grows in size and in power in order to drive the blood through the greatly increased area of cir-

Management of Pregnancy

culation; her lungs work harder to purify this blood; her whole digestive system works harder to elaborate the nourishment that has to be supplied; and her kidneys and other organs have also to put in an extra amount of work to carry off effete material and to maintain the balance of the income and expenditure of the body. It has been well said that pregnancy is the supreme test of soundness of structure and health of function.

The balance between a normal and an abnormal pregnancy is delicate, and the physiological state constantly borders on the pathological; therefore it is the more necessary that the pregnant woman should have adequate and suitable food, pure air, pure water, ample opportunities for rest, for sleep, and for exercise. No violent change needs to be made in a well-ordered life. It would be a great mistake for the expectant mother to regard herself as an invalid whose food must be specially considered and who should lay aside her usual duties and activities. The woman's sense of her ability to work should be the measure of her work, and her feeling of fatigue should be the signal for rest. Of course, this is a counsel of perfection, and it is quite evident that large numbers of women—indeed, the majority of women—are prevented by the circumstances of their lives and the nature of their work from commanding ideal conditions during pregnancy. It is, however, equally true that a large number of women could arrange their lives better than they do : that rich women in society might quite well live a life of comparative retirement ; while poor women who are burdened with the cares of house ánd family ought to be relieved, if necessary by the action of the State, from the necessity of strenuous outside work during these most exacting months.

The value of the child-bearing woman and of her offspring has recently been forced on the attention of the nation, and it is to be hoped that both law and custom may be so modified by the new appreciation of the value of motherhood that her burdens may be considerably reduced.

After all, there are certain precautions that could be taken by all pregnant women. They might all avoid alcohol, which in its stronger forms is positively injurious to their health, and they might endeavour to procure the proper action of their skin by washing and by friction, and also secure the adequate function both of the kidneys and of the bowels. The pregnant woman should remember that in her condition there is a considerable diversion of nervous energy to the needs of the growing uterus and child, and that this, in addition to a constantly increasing mechanical pressure, may lead to an increasing difficulty in the functions of her other organs. It is certain that some of the diseases of pregnancy and many of the discomforts of that state depend on the overloading of the system with the worn-out or partly worn-out products of digestion. These ought to be got rid of, but they linger in the body owing to the sluggishness of the excretory organs. Women are much tempted to secure relief from discomfort by the use of drugs ; this is to be deprecated, and an effort should be made to secure brisk and efficient action by means of variety in diet, the substitution of wholemeal or brown bread for ordinary white bread, and the use of a greater abundance of vegetables and fruits instead of butcher's meat.

Exercise is also a real help to excretion. During exercise the different parts of the body to a certain extent massage themselves, for there is a variation of pressure here and pressure there which tends to the improvement of the circulation and therefore to the capacity for elimination.

The pregnant woman should be very careful strictly to limit stimulants, not only alcohol, but also the much more generally abused stimulants containing *theine* and *caffeine*. These powerful alkaloids, found in tea and coffee, are frequently taken to excess, and, with the indigestible bitter extractives that abound in tea that has stood too long, are very apt to produce both over-stimulation and indigestion. The expectant mother should drink freely of water, either hot or cold, barley water, and occasionally of lemonade and similar drinks.

Clothing.—Clothing should be warm, light and adequate. The whole surface of the body should be covered, and care be taken that, as far as possible, the clothes should exercise no injurious pressure and should be capable of adjustment to the increasing size and altering figure. It is advisable that petticoats should be made with bodices instead of bands, so as to distribute their weight and to transfer it largely from the waist to the shoulders. Women who have been in the habit of wearing corsets would probably be uncomfortable if they left off these supports, but the corsets, if worn, must be adapted to the circumstances. Many excellent special corsets are made by outfitters with ingenious contrivances to let them out as pregnancy advances, but for those women who cannot afford such luxuries much relief may be afforded by procuring a larger pair of very soft, pliable stays which can be laced down the back with three-cord white silk elastic, and are susceptible of letting out between the side seams and the front by long slits furnished with eyelet-holes, which also should be laced with the silk elastic.

The shoes should be comfortably adapted to the feet, the toes not too pointed and the heels low and broad. Pegtop heels are never either beautiful or likely to secure a graceful carriage

Management of Pregnancy

and a comfortable foot, but during pregnancy high narrow heels are a positive danger, and not only lead to discomfort but sometimes to an awkward fall, which may inflict very serious injury on both mother and child.

The duties of the married state during pregnancy. — Amongst the important questions of the hygiene of pregnancy is the relation of the woman to her husband. It has been customary of late, especially by American authors, to advise married couples to lead single lives from the commencement of pregnancy to the end of lactation. This may perhaps be a counsel of perfection, and certainly it complies with the rule of the Roman Catholic Church. It is, however, to be remembered that one of the objects of matrimony was the avoidance of sin, and it would be very inconsiderate to ask a husband to live a single life for, say, eighteen months at a time. Every married couple must settle the ecclesiastical question for themselves, but from a medical point of view no harm will be done to the woman by a moderate fulfilment of the duties of matrimony. During the early weeks of pregnancy —especially in a first pregnancy —if the wife is feeling sick and uncomfortable, good sense will certainly lead both her and her husband to abstain, and in all cases it is the wife who must decide whether or not she feels able and willing to discharge the duties of the married

99

The Seven Ages of Woman

state. From the time that the tendency to sickness subsides it is probable that a more regular use may be made of this gift. Later on, during the last three months of pregnancy, most women will find that they require a complete holiday, and then no demands should be made on them. The whole matter needs to be regulated by mutual forbearance and by common sense, but there is no reason to fear, as some authors have lately taught us to fear, that any harm will accrue to the fœtus *in utero* by intercourse between the husband and wife.

CHAPTER V

PREPARATION FOR LABOUR

In one sense the preparation for labour begins with pregnancy, and consists in the careful observance of all the rules of hygiene and of a gradual adaptation of the woman's work, exercise, and rest to her changing condition. But the preparation for labour to be considered in this chapter is the more immediate preparation which ought to be undertaken during the last few weeks before the expected birth of the child.

Preparation of the house.—It is well, when it is possible to arrange for it, that the house should be set in order, and especially that the drains and water supply should be tested. Much illness is caused by inadequately trapped and ill-ventilated drains, and also much evil is caused by the neglect to secure a supply of pure water. Practically this means that a reliable surveyor should test the drains and that the water used for household purposes should be examined at a laboratory. I shall be reminded at once that these are counsels of perfection; but, at any rate, with regard to the water supply, a rough and ready test is to fill a white glass water jug with freshly drawn water and to add to it a few drops of Condy's fluid, enough to give the water a faint pink tinge. The jug should be carefully covered over to keep out the dust, and should stand on a sheet of white paper for five or six hours. If at the end of that time the delicate pink tinge remains the water may be considered to be free from the more dangerous forms of organic impurities. If, however, the pink tinge has given place to a faintly yellowish or brownish hue, the water is not free from contamination, and if no better supply can be procured it must be boiled before it is consumed.

Preparation of the birth chamber.— In houses where there are one or more spare rooms special preparation should be made for the confinement, and if possible two rooms, one opening out of the other, should be set apart for the use of the mother, nurse, and baby. These rooms should receive a thorough " spring cleaning " : the ceilings and walls should be cleaned, carpets should be taken up, and the floor scrubbed, or waxed and polished, according to circumstances. Clean window curtains should be put up, and the window blinds should be cleaned or washed. All unnecessary furniture should be removed from the lying-in chamber, and heavy articles of furniture, such as wardrobes, should have their tops very thoroughly wiped over with a cloth wet with 1 in 20 carbolic lotion. No soiled linen

Preparation for Labour

basket and no boot-rack should remain in the room. If any rugs are to be retained in the birth chamber they must be thoroughly beaten and then rubbed over with carbolic lotion. There should be two single beds in the lying-in chamber, because it is a great relief and comfort to the patient to be lifted from one bed to another night and morning, and also because the nursing is both easier and more efficient when the patient is on a narrow bed. The bed must be firm but not too hard —a hair mattress over a palliasse or wire-chain mattress would be very comfortable. A large sheet of waterproof cloth should cover the entire mattress, tucked in at the head and feet so as to prevent it from wrinkling ; over this a perfectly clean blanket should be smoothly laid and covered in the usual way with a sheet. The centre of the bed should be further protected by a sheet of india-rubber cloth about 8 feet wide, long enough to tuck in on either side, and this in its turn should be covered by a sheet folded lengthwise, also tucked in at each side. The ordinary top sheet and necessary blankets must be perfectly clean, fresh from wash or new.

Until the bed is required for use it should be covered with a large clean dust-sheet to prevent any accidental contamination. It is impossible to insist too strongly that all sheets, pillow cases, blankets, coverlets, and other objects shall be absolutely clean, and that those which are kept in reserve shall be carefully stored in drawers or on shelves well covered in and tucked over by clean linen. It is the more necessary to insist on this, because occasionally even an experienced nurse will commit some blunder which under the circumstances amounts to a crime, and forget the scrupulous cleanliness that is necessary to the patient's welfare. Sometimes piles of clean linen may be seen lying about a room exposed to dust and dirt, or, worse still, laid on the floor, where they are sure to be soiled and perhaps even trodden upon.

It is very convenient that in the lying-in room there should be a small cupboard or covered shelf on which medicines, medicine glasses, and feeding cups can be arranged; it is also convenient, where practicable, that the room should be near the bath-room and lavatory, in order to secure both a ready supply of hot and cold water and also the desirable facility for the immediate emptying of slop water, bed-pans, etc. It is true that all these conveniences cannot be procured in every house, but it is well to set a high standard towards which everyone can work.

If possible, there should be a wardrobe or chest of drawers in the lying-in chamber, or in the room next to it, entirely devoted to the bed linen and personal linen of the patient, and where also all the baby's requisites can be stored.

Of course, where possible, it is very desirable

that the patient should have a clean nightgown every day, but even when this cannot be secured the nightgown should be changed every twelve hours, the discarded garment being hung up to air and to purify until it is again needed for use.

When the patient is able to sit up she will need a dressing jacket, which should always be of washing material.

Besides nightgowns and dressing jackets, the patient will need binders. There are many good patterns on the market, but for simplicity and efficiency there is nothing better than the *many-tailed abdominal bandage*. This has been made fairly familiar to all people who have worked at Red Cross and other nursing centres during the War. It consists of a piece of soft muslin or calico about 15 inches square, on which are laid four or five strips of elastic flannel, or domett, about 5 inches wide and 1 yard to 1¼ yards in length. These should be stitched on to the central piece, each overlapping about one-third. Should this form of bandage be unobtainable, it suffices to have a supply of ordinary roller towels, which can be used double and secured round the patient's body with safety-pins.

The baby's requirements at birth are few and simple. It must have a bed in which to sleep, and the time-honoured bed is always known as a *berceaunette* or *bassinette*. The old English cradle was made of wood, which was more liable to harbour insects and dust; but apparently the idea of the wicker-work bassinette (more easily kept clean and better ventilated) came to us from France, and now, in many instances, a further improvement has been made of an enamelled iron framework with a hammock of cotton or linen netting.

The baby's bed must be comfortably warm but not too soft, and there should be an adequate arrangement for protecting the child's head from draughts and its eyes from the light. The baby needs no sheets, but a sufficient supply of soft, clean blankets. A little pillow is customary, and in India infants appear to derive much advantage from a pair of tiny pillows four or five inches in diameter, which are laid the length of the cradle and support the back; they are, however, seldom seen in England.

The baby's basket, even though not an absolute necessity, is a great convenience to the nurse, because in it she can keep the many little oddments that are used in a baby's toilet, not only its clothes, but its powder, a small tube of cold cream or white vaseline, needles, thread, safety-pins, etc.

Baby's clothes.—A baby's clothes should be simple and easy to put on. Every woman has her own ideas on this subject, and whatever is recommended is quite sure to be criticised; but for the benefit of the few young mothers who

Preparation for Labour

have no mother or mother-in-law to help them in such matters, one may furnish the following list : —

Four very elastic flannel binders, 5½ inches wide and 24 inches long. These, if desired, may be made on the " many-tail " principle—two strands.

Four fine soft vests, open either down front or back.

Three or four flannel petticoats with bodices, 31 inches in length from waist to hem.

Six or eight day gowns and the same number of night-gowns, made either of fine cotton or fine woollen material, high to the neck, with sleeves to the wrist, and about 27 to 32 inches in length from the neck to the hem, open all the way down the back. No petticoats or dresses are really necessary, but most mothers like to provide them. They may be made according to taste, but it is very desirable that they should not be too elaborate nor too long.

Four squares at least, known as head flannels, two more or less embroidered, and two simply bound with white silk ribbon, for use at night.

Four dozen diapers, some of which should be of Turkish towelling or of butter muslin, 1 yard square (double thickness).

One waterproof pilch.

Two over-flannels or flannel drawers.

In addition to these garments, which should be provided beforehand, the baby will require either a cloak or a shawl and a hood for outdoor wear. This hood may simply be made of an ordinary silk or cambric handkerchief, folded in such a way as to form a Dutch bonnet—this for convenience of washing.

PART III

THE YOUNG MOTHER

CHAPTER I

SIGNS AND SYMPTOMS OF THE THREE STAGES OF LABOUR

THERE are three stages in labour. The first of them lasts from the commencement of the opening of the mouth of the neck of the womb—which frequently, but not invariably, coincides with the beginning of painful contractions—up to the full dilatation of the mouth, which generally corresponds to the " escape of the waters."

The second stage begins with the " escape of the waters " and ends with the birth of the child.

The third stage commences with the birth of the child and ends with the expulsion of the placenta or afterbirth.

First stage.—In many cases, before the onset of true labour, there is a preparatory stage which may not be much noticed by the mother. The painless contractions of the womb which occur all through pregnancy become stronger as the time of labour approaches, and may even be felt by the mother's hands laid on her abdomen. In some cases this stage is accompanied by colicky pains. The premonitory pains are very generally caused by constipation and flatulent distension of the bowels, and are irregular in point of time and in severity. They are chiefly of importance because an inexperienced patient thinks that they are true labour pains, and if they happen in the night she is likely to be unduly alarmed, and to fear that even if the nurse be in the house the doctor will not reach her in time. It is well, therefore, to contrast the premonitory or false pains with those of the first stage of true labour.

True labour pains begin in the back and extend round to the front of the abdomen ; they are rhythmic in character—that is to say, they occur at more or less regular intervals, and begin gently, almost imperceptibly, attain a maximum of intensity, and then rather more rapidly decline, leaving the patient quite comfortable until the next pain commences. The false pains, on the other hand, are entirely abdominal, they greatly resemble the pains that are caused by the action of aperient medicine, they have no rhythmic character, they last indefinitely, and are probably entirely cured by a dose of castor oil or an efficient enema.

Another phenomenon during this preparatory stage, which usually announces preparation for the dilatation of the mouth of the neck of the womb, consists in the discharge of more or less mucus, which is sometimes slightly blood-stained. The mucus is derived from the plug that has gradually formed in the canal of the neck of the womb, and the tinge of blood in it is due to the breaking of minute vessels in that part. These so-called *false pains* are apt to recur during the two or three days immediately preceding labour, and frequently give rise to a mistaken idea on the part of the patient that her labour has lasted several days. An experienced nurse—or the doctor if present—should explain the real condition of affairs to the patient, so that she may be more cheerful and have no unnecessary fears as to the probable effects of her discomfort.

True labour begins when the mouth of the womb commences to dilate, and may be identified, as said before, by the rhythmical character and gradually increasing intensity of the pains. The nurse in attendance ought to be able to recognise them, and should send for the doctor in order that the patient's condition may be properly ascertained and any necessary treatment advised and carried into effect.

The commencement of labour is sometimes accompanied by sickness; this should not cause any anxiety or alarm, for not only is it natural, but it is also beneficial, because it tends to assist the necessary dilatation of the mouth of the womb.

First Stage of Labour

When labour begins, certain preparations should be made. If the patient has not already had a dose of castor oil or some other efficient and painless aperient, it should now be administered. A tablespoonful is a good average dose. It may be taken floating on lemon juice, shaken up with hot coffee, or in the form of an emulsion (Appendix, Formula 1). Failing these methods, one of the nicest and readiest ways is to blunt the sense of taste by sucking a piece of ice or a strong peppermint, then to swallow the oil from a spoon and to resume the sucking of ice or peppermint. This method prevents the patient from appreciating the disagreeable flavour of the oil and its still more disagreeable clamminess. The one method to be avoided is the taking of the oil floating on brandy or whisky. The small amount of stimulant might perhaps be harmless, but the action of the spirit on the oil is very apt to cause eructations, and a disagreeable after-taste which lasts for a considerable time.

As soon as the oil has been swallowed the patient should have a warm bath at a temperature of about 100° F. She is not to lie and soak in the water, for that would probably cause undesirable relaxation and lassitude, but she should have a thorough good wash of the whole body, finishing up by sponging herself all over with fresh water. After the bath clean clothes should be put on, and the nightgown should be pinned up to prevent it from being soiled while she is still able to walk about, and over this a clean washable petticoat and a dressing-gown. When the patient returns to her bedroom the nurse should brush and plait her hair in two tails so that she can lie comfortably on either side or on her back without a mass of hair pressing on her head and causing headache. These preparations made, the patient may, if she wishes, take a little light refreshment, tea or coffee, with bread and butter or toast, or a cup of clear soup, Bovril, etc. No really solid food should be taken, because the digestive powers are probably in abeyance, and also because sickness is not an infrequent accompaniment of labour.

It is by no means necessary that the patient should go to bed or lie down during the first stage of labour. It is better for her cheerfulness, and also for the progress of the necessary dilatation, that she should walk, sit, or stand, as she pleases, and it is also far better for her that she should employ herself, the one restriction being that she is not to read medical books or nursing manuals! The young mother will probably find that whatever she is doing she has to stop from time to time as the pains come on. During the early part of the process the pains are usually neither long nor severe, but as time goes on she will find that they are more frequent, of longer duration, and more difficult to bear. It is, however, greatly to be desired that she should do her best to be brave and cheerful, to bear each pain as it comes, remembering that every painful contraction of the womb accomplishes a certain amount of work, and therefore brings her nearer to the end of her troubles and the fruition of her hopes. The more reasonable, the more courageous, and the more cheerful she is, the more nervous energy will she have, and therefore the shorter and more propitious will be her labour. Women who give way to low spirits and to hysterical crying and sobbing greatly increase their own trouble, and add unnecessarily to the mental sufferings of their husbands and friends.

The length of the first stage varies very greatly. In the case of a vigorous young woman with a well-shaped pelvis and a child of ordinary size and weight, and who is possessed of good muscular and nervous power, the process may be of a few hours' duration only. On the other hand, in cases where there is disproportion between the child and the pelvis, and in those cases where the woman is feeble, or flabby in nerve and muscle, the truly natural process of labour will be greatly handicapped, and the contractions may be feeble and inefficient, although more than ordinarily painful. These are the considerations that make one anxious that every expectant mother should have loving care during pregnancy, and should also do her best to secure for herself health and efficiency of body and a serene and courageous mind.

From this it is also evident that the doctor should have seen the patient during her pregnancy, so that the relative size of passages and passenger shall be known, and that proper means may be used to make the solution of the problem, "passages, passenger, and power," easy. The average duration of the first stage for a first labour is twenty-four hours, but it is evident, from what has been said above, that this does not mean twenty-four hours of pain. On the contrary, when the first stage is long and slow the patient is generally able to obtain intervals of sleep or rest, and can take a sufficiency of simple food.

Second stage. —That the second stage of labour is imminent may be judged by the dilating pains becoming very frequent, prolonged, and painful. By this time the patient will generally have taken to bed, although she need not yet assume any special position. Coincidently with the completion of sufficient dilatation of the mouth and neck of the womb to permit of the passage of the child there will generally be a free flow of watery fluid from the vagina. This is due to the rupture of the bag of membranes in which the baby is enclosed. A clever nurse can very generally guess when this event is imminent, and by holding a sterilised bowl in a convenient position she can catch the greater part of the fluid and so save the swamping of the draw-sheet which would otherwise occur.

Immediately the second stage has commenced the patient experiences a little interval of comparative ease and a great sense of relief so far as pressure and breathing are concerned. The respite, however, is short. Painful contractions soon recommence, but their character is changed. Women frequently compare the pains of the first stage either to toothache or to the colicky pains caused by the action of an aperient. The pains in the second stage are usually compared to the sensations of tearing and rending which accompany the passage of a very large and constipated motion. The pains are more massive in character and really more severe, but all mothers agree that they are more easy to bear than those of the first stage. There is a comforting sense that something definite is accomplished by each pain, and therefore, while the suffering is greater, so, too, is the capacity for bearing it.

The commencement of the second stage, like that of the first, is frequently accompanied by a fit of vomiting, which in this instance also is natural and helpful. The process may be repeated two or three times, and need give rise to no anxiety, but frequently repeated and virtually incessant vomiting needs a doctor's treatment.

The Seven Ages of Woman

During the second stage the patient should remain in bed, but she may still choose her own position. Apparently labour advances somewhat more rapidly when she is lying on her back, but the difference that this makes to the whole labour is slight and may be disregarded. If things are going well there is no need to trouble the patient with food or medicine. It is, however, necessary that the nurse should ascertain from time to time that everything is scrupulously clean, she should arrange the clothes to her patient's convenience, and take particular care that the nightgown does not become soiled by the inevitable discharge. She must also watch that the bladder does not become loaded; she must remind the patient to empty it from time to time, and should this become impossible owing to the pressure of the descending head she must draw the water off by means of a well-boiled elastic catheter, taking particular care to cleanse the orifice of the urethra and all the adjacent parts before she introduces it. Should the catheter unfortunately become soiled it must be washed and reboiled before it is passed into the bladder. It is absolutely necessary that the nurse should see what she is doing. The old-fashioned idea that it is nursing etiquette to pass the catheter without looking is a very foolish one, and has frequently led to the unintentional soiling of the catheter and to the consequent infection of the bladder—a very tiresome accident to both nurse and patient. Every sensible woman will recognise that the truest modesty and refinement are shown not by a covering up of the body, but by a simple compliance with all necessary nursing attentions.

It not infrequently happens that towards the end of the second stage fæces are forced out, owing to the pressure of the infant's head on the bowel. The patient at this time is probably under chloroform and knows nothing of what is happening. The nurse or doctor, however, must be vigilant, and immediately remove all contaminating matter and thoroughly wash and disinfect all parts adjacent to the anus and vulva.

Throughout the second stage the child's head is gradually forced through the pelvis, and towards its close it lies on the pelvic floor. The pains then become redoubled in force, frequency, and length. Even if chloroform has not been necessary before, its administration at this stage is of great advantage. Not only does it abolish the patient's sense of pain, but it diminishes the risk of laceration, partly by overcoming spasm and rigidity in the soft parts, and partly by diminishing the violence of the uterine contractions, which sometimes urge the head too strongly forwards. It is seldom that the anæsthetic needs to be given to the surgical extent. As a rule, a little chloroform poured on a layer of cotton wool lying in the bottom of a tumbler can be held by the patient herself. As she inhales the vapour of the chloroform and her sense of pain is dulled, or lost, her hold on the tumbler relaxes, and it falls into the bed. The nurse picks it up and has it ready with a few more drops of chloroform ready for the next pain. In all ordinary cases this simple and partial anæsthesia is sufficient, but in cases where there is need for a deeper anæsthesia the presence of a skilled anæsthetist is desirable. In many parts of the Mission Field, and in many parts of the Dominions and Colonies, where young English mothers have to bear their first child, the services of a second doctor may not be available, but many nurses have been trained to administer chloroform; they frequently do it well; and, anyhow, under these circumstances, the choice lies between the nurse's administration and the very partial relief that the patient is able to afford to herself.

Recently a different method of anæsthesia in which pain is annulled by the administration of morphia and scopolamine has been greatly commended. In ordinary cases in England the choice of the anæsthetic, like all other professional details, must be left to the doctor, and it is at present an open question with the profession whether this form of anæsthesia is in any way superior to that procured by chloroform or ether.

Second Stage of Labour

It is, however, certain that the old-fashioned way is safe and efficient, and that the patient will do well to confide herself entirely to the doctor of her choice.

Just at the close of the second stage the uterine efforts succeed each other with scarcely any intermission. The perineum becomes more and more distended and the anus gapes widely. The whole ring of the vulva is also stretched to its greatest extent, and the top of the baby's head becomes more and more visible. Advance and recession continue, until finally there is an advance followed by no recession, and then another effort or two accomplishes the delivery of the head. Whoever is in attendance on the mother should wipe the baby's eyes, nose, and mouth to clear away mucus and discharge; a finger should also be passed round the child's neck to ascertain that it is not being strangled by a tight loop of the umbilical cord. If a loop is found which is not tight it may be left alone, but if it appears to be inconveniencing the child it should be gently loosened. No effort should be made to accelerate the process of the birth by pulling on the child's head; the nurse should press gently but steadily downwards and backwards on the upper part of the child as felt through the mother's abdomen. After a short pause the uterus again takes up its labours, one shoulder of the child appears under the pubic arch, the infant's face turns a little from the mother's back towards her thigh, the second shoulder slips over the edge of the perineum, and the body and legs of the child follow rapidly.

The duty of the attendant is to wait on nature and neither to thwart nor unduly to assist. The child's head and body should be carefully guided forwards towards the mother's abdomen in order to relieve the strain on her sensitive structures, and the steady downward and backward pressure on the abdomen should be maintained even after the birth is completed.

Directly the baby is born the administration of chloroform must be stopped and the mother must be gently turned on to her back. Her knees should be supported in the bent position, and the baby should be so placed that it cannot injure its mother by kicking and also that it runs no risk of injury or suffocation.

Third stage.—The third stage of labour now commences. It consists in the expulsion of the *placenta* or *afterbirth*. In many cases this organ is detached from the wall of the uterus by one of the pains which complete the second stage, and it may follow the birth of the child very rapidly. In other cases the uterus has to contract again and again to complete its detachment. The patient will then experience recurrent pains, nothing like so severe as those of the second stage, but frequently in her half-dazed condition she will demand chloroform. This must not be given, for its influence would tend to relax the womb, to stop its contractions, and therefore to delay the birth of the placenta and also to favour the occurrence of hæmorrhage. The afterbirth must not be pulled away. Gentle massage of the abdomen will stimulate the uterus and assist its contractions, and as a rule nothing more is necessary.

The time occupied by the third stage varies from a few minutes to half an hour or more, but it is seldom prolonged more than twenty minutes after the birth of the child.

In exceptional cases the placenta, although detached from the womb, is retained within it. Doctors and midwives know well how to deal with this condition, but where unfortunately neither is present and this accident occurs, a small teaspoonful of the liquid extract of ergot, or a tabloid containing a grain of ergot in may be administered in plenty of cold water. Sometimes, but fortunately very rarely, the natural separation of the placenta from the wall of the uterus does not occur, and it may be necessary for the doctor to remove it. It is usual in such cases to anæsthetise the patient so that she may be spared all unnecessary pain and the doctor may work under more favourable conditions.

The time at which the connection of the infant with its mother ought to be severed depends upon circumstances. So long as the navel cord pulsates the child is benefited by its connection, but when pulsation ceases, or sooner should the child be very blue in the face or not breathing properly, the cord should be tied and cut. The first tie should be about 8 inches from the child's body, and the second 2 inches further on. The division should be made with a pair of round-pointed scissors, and great care should be taken that in cutting the cord no injury be done to the child's fingers or other parts of its body.

CHAPTER II

CARE OF THE YOUNG MOTHER

PROBABLY life holds no more blissful moment for a woman than that which succeeds to the end of labour. The sudden cessation of pain, the relief of anxiety, and the joy that "a man is born into the world," all combine to give her complete satisfaction. Even the natural feeling of weariness tends rather to enhance than to diminish her comfort. It is very essential that complete rest and quiet should be secured. In many patients who are naturally vigorous and who are not too greatly fatigued there is a temptation to chatter, to discuss the events of the labour, and to express natural admiration of the baby. The strictest quiet is, however, indicated, and all excitement must be avoided as far as is possible.

Directly the third stage is completed the mother must be turned on her left side with the knees well drawn up, and all soiled clothing must be gently withdrawn. The vulva and adjacent parts should then be rapidly but gently washed and dried. The margin of the vulva and the perineum should be examined. In all first deliveries a certain small amount of laceration will be found. The anterior edge of the perineum will probably be notched, and in some cases the laceration extends farther back; indeed, after a difficult or too rapid a delivery, the tissues may be torn through into the bowel. In cases where there is more than the merest notch the doctor will have to pass one or more sutures, preferably of silkworm gut or silver wire. Catgut sutures melt too rapidly, and silk and thread are far from aseptic in this position. In other cases, where no stitching is necessary, it suffices to anoint the margins of the vulva with an aseptic ointment (Appendix, Formula 2). A fresh draw-sheet or accouchement sheet should be laid under the patient, the vulva should be covered with a sanitary towel or pad of gamgee tissue, and the clean nightgown should be unpinned and drawn down over her knees; it should not be drawn down behind, because it would certainly become soiled. The binder should now be accurately adjusted, but not drawn too tight.

If the patient be inclined for a little nourishment she may have any simple ordinary food, such as milk, Benger's food, cornflour, etc., or, if she prefers it, a cup of tea or coffee, soup, or Bovril. It is very seldom that drugs are needed at this stage, but should the pulse remain over 100, or should the discharge be too profuse, the doctor may perhaps order a dose of ergot (a small teaspoonful to a wineglassful of water, or a one-grain tabloid of ergotin).

The room should then be darkened, and the patient should do her best to get to sleep, or at any rate to remain silent and at perfect rest.

In old-fashioned times a great point was made of the mother retaining the absolutely recumbent position for some days after delivery, and it was generally required that she should lie very still for a week or ten days. It is now recognised that the recumbent position permits the accumulation of discharge in the vagina, and therefore, as soon as the patient has had her first rest or sleep, she is to be propped into a comfortable reclining position, and kept there without muscular exertion by means of some sort of sling or hammock ; a perfectly efficient one can be contrived by means of an old sterilised sheet folded lengthways, passed under the patient's knees, and secured to the head of the bed on each side.

After a few days it is very desirable that the patient should be encouraged to do some exercises lying in bed. She may roll from side to side, and may gently raise or lower each leg alternately. These exercises should be supplemented by gentle massage, especially of the abdomen, twice a day. Careful attention should be paid to the condition of the uterus, and it will be found that daily massage of this organ will help to maintain its tone, and will therefore prevent the accumulation in it of bloodclots and discharge, so averting the tendency to sepsis and accelerating the return of the organ to its normal condition.

The temperature and pulse should be taken every six hours during the first week, for abnormalities in their condition constitute the most valuable danger signal, and call the attention of both doctor and nurse to the possible commencement of trouble. Immediately after delivery the temperature may be a few points above normal, and the pulse slightly quickened; but in a few hours both should have returned to their normal standard. In the case of most women in their first labour, and in all women who have any difficulty with their breasts, a rise of temperature may be expected on the third evening, and accompanying this rise there may be a little acceleration of pulse. The breasts will be found at this time to be full, turgid, and hard. They ought to be covered with wool and carefully supported by a bandage, preferably a many-tailed bandage; the lower tails come from the back under the arms and cross in front, while one or two of the upper tails come over the shoulders and are secured to the lower by safety-pins; thus the breasts are supported as in a sling. If all goes well milk soon begins to flow, the turgidity subsides, and the pulse and temperature chart become normal. Much depends on

Care of the Young Mother

the wisdom shown by the nurse and on the cheerful collaboration of the patient. The baby should be put to the breast from the very first, but it should not be allowed to spend much useless effort in seeking milk before it is sufficiently secreted. In nearly all first cases the baby will require some artificial feeding for the first two or three days, but the food must never be administered with a spoon; the child must be encouraged to work for its living, and should suck its food through a teat which permits the flow of milk with not more facility than does the human nipple.

It is very important that the infant should be put to the breast regularly, but it is equally important that the feeds should not be too frequent. The old rule of feeding once in two hours for the first month is now held accountable for the great difficulty and strain experienced by most women in lactation. It is also probably responsible for the fact that many women are unable to suckle their children at all, and that many more are compelled to abandon the attempt about the fourth or fifth week.

If the bladder has been kept empty during labour there is seldom any need to trouble about its function immediately after delivery; probably an interval of five, or even six, hours may safely elapse before sufficient urine has accumulated to demand the evacuation of the bladder.

The Seven Ages of Woman

The performance of the function, however, must not be subject to the patient's sensations. Owing to the pressure on the bladder, especially on its neck, towards the end of the second stage of labour, it is somewhat numb, and does not readily appreciate the collection within it of urine. The nurse should feel the lower part of the abdomen and suggest micturition when the bladder appears to be full; also in the event of the uterus seeming to be relaxed and too large. An overfull bladder diverts nervous energy from the uterus and leads to its undue relaxation. The nurse should slip a well warmed and disinfected bedpan under the patient's hips, and should encourage her to make the necessary effort. Some women are marvellously stupid about the use of the bedpan. As a matter of fact, their alleged inability to use it is entirely nervous, and if only they could make up their minds to relax the neck of the bladder, the urine would flow of its own accord, but in cases where an undue fuss and worry develop it is far better that the nurse should pass the catheter rather than the bladder should remain overfull or the patient be irritated and nervous.

The bowels, having been thoroughly cleared before and during labour, will probably not act of their own accord for some few days, but considering the difficulty of defæcation in the horizontal position and the probable slight upset incident to the first secretion of milk, it is wise to give a grain or two of extract of cascara, a vegetable laxative pill, or some other simple aperient every night from the beginning. Should these means fail to produce a free evacuation, on the morning of the third day an oil enema may be given (Appendix, Formula 8).

For the rest of the lying-in period this treatment may be continued, or a daily evacuation may be solicited by means of glycerin, or, still better, of a cacao-butter suppository introduced into the bowel every morning.

The patient's food should be abundant, but light and nourishing. She should not have much meat, no flatulent vegetables, or raw fruit, but an abundance of milky food, bread, butter, eggs, and stewed fruit. It is desirable that the meals should as far as possible be given at the hours to which she is accustomed, for it is to be carefully remembered that her condition is one of health, not of disease, and her diet should be as far as possible on normal lines.

Every case of confinement must, of course, be managed according to the orders of the doctor in charge, and every circumstance connected with the health of the patient and the baby must be reported at once. Neither nurse nor patient must disobey the doctor, for by so doing they take upon themselves a responsibility which they are not fitted to bear.

The Seven Ages of Woman

Puerperal sepsis.—Puerperal fever or sepsis is always due to certain germs capable of causing sepsis having gained access to the woman's tissues.

Although prolonged and difficult labour may increase the patient's danger by depressing her vitality and so making her tissues a suitable soil, yet the germs must be sown, or they could not grow. The infection may be conveyed by the hands of doctor or nurse, by dirty instruments, such as an enema syringe, or by soiled clothes or bed-linen. Sometimes the infection appears to be already in the patient's system, as in cases where puerperal sepsis attacks a woman who is suffering from pneumonia, influenza, decayed teeth, septic tonsils, or whitlow, or in whom some portion of placenta or membranes remains in the uterus.

In any case, the chief symptoms are rise of temperature, sense of illness, headache, furred tongue, and loss of appetite. The condition grows rapidly worse, and unless treatment is early, wise, and vigorous the end is rapid. Peritonitis may set in, or other manifestations of sepsis appear, and the patient dies within a few days of the commencement of the symptoms.

This is an illustration of how irreparable injury may ensue from want of simple and easy precautions. The patient is lost from carelessness, not from inevitable ill fortune.

Care of the Young Mother

Notification and registration of birth. — Every birth must be notified by the father, or by someone who was present at the event, within forty-eight hours, and the child must be registered within six weeks.

The Notification of Births Act has just been made compulsory, and indicates a very valuable advance in the national care of infant life. Among the poorer classes a large percentage of infants die within the first few days of life. In many cases this mortality is inevitable; the child has been born in such a state of weakness or disease that it is unable to maintain an independent existence; but in other cases the fatality is due to avoidable causes, and the sympathetic help of the Health Visitor may be effectual in saving the infant's life.

Again, notification of birth is a great safeguard against the disastrous effects of *ophthalmia neonatorum* (sore eyes). This malady is due to infection of the child's eyes during the process of birth or immediately afterwards. The infection is virulent, and unless the eyes are properly treated in the beginning blindness is the all too probable result. Even the children of the well-to-do may suffer in this way, but in their case the first signs of mischief are recognised by nurse and by doctor, and sight is usually preserved by appropriate treatment.

CHAPTER III

ABNORMAL PREGNANCY

Miscarriage.—As we have seen in the chapter dealing with menstruation, ovulation occurs approximately once in twenty-eight days, and although during pregnancy this function of the ovaries is more or less in abeyance, it is not entirely abolished. There is therefore a possible awakening of the ovarian influence every fourth week, and it is at this time that the uterus is most disposed to eject its contents. Normally nothing happens, and the woman is absolutely unconscious that there is the smallest tendency towards premature evacuation of the womb. When any abnormal condition exists and the vitality of the ovum is in any way threatened, it is natural that the additional factor of ovarian activity should reinforce the morbid condition, and this is the reason why miscarriage is prone to occur at the eighth, twelfth, sixteenth, and twentieth weeks rather than at the seventh, thirteenth, or nineteenth.

The determining causes of miscarriage are morbid conditions affecting the mother or the ovum. Unhealthy influences existing in the father count for little except so far as they first affect the wife.

Among the commonest causes of miscarriage —and, indeed, perhaps the commonest cause — in the later months of pregnancy is syphilis. A man who has suffered from this disease, and who marries believing that he is cured, may yet have the poison latent in his tissues. The wife becomes infected, and probably the symptoms that might draw her attention to the fact are so slight that the trouble goes on unrecognised, unsuspected, and therefore untreated, but none the less sufficiently potent to destroy or to endanger the life of the embryo. A miscarriage occurs, and is readily attributed, both by patient and doctor, to over-fatigue, or to some slight accident, and so the true cause escapes detection. The patient still shows no evident symptoms of disease, and it is not until several miscarriages have occurred that the doctor, at any rate, becomes suspicious, and diagnosis and treatment follow. If the treatment be effectual the next pregnancy will probably come to a successful termination.

In some instances the evil influence of syphilis decreases in power, and even if it is untreated, after several miscarriages or premature births a child is born at full term. This child may, however, be stillborn owing to the disease, or, having been born alive, it may die within a few days.

The Seven Ages of Woman

Unfortunately, the mischief caused by syphilis does not end when at last a child is able to survive its birth. A very large number of infants die within the first year from its effects. These are the children who are described as *marasmic* babies, or " wasters " ; they are miserable, ill-nourished little creatures, with dull, yellow-grey skins, and grotesquely senile or monkey-like faces. Very frequently they have rashes about the buttocks and other parts of the body, sores or fissures about the angles of the mouth, and a peculiar bossy condition of the bones of the forehead. These poor little mites appear to be unable to obtain nourishment from their food, they do not grow and prosper, and they furnish a large number of the victims of meningitis. It is scarcely desirable that they should survive ; at the same time it is to be remembered that suitable treatment is very effectual in this disease.

Another cause of miscarriage is to be found in the infection of other zymotic diseases, more especially the eruptive fevers, such as smallpox, scarlet fever, and measles. In the same category of miscarriages caused by poisons derived from the blood of the mother we must place those that occur in the course or after an attack of cholera or influenza. In these and in all similar cases the death of the embryo or injury to the tissues of the ovum is the efficient cause of the miscarriage. A dead embryo, or membranes and placenta that are spoiled, and inadequate to perform their functions, cause the contents of the uterus to become a "foreign body." The circulation of blood between the embryo and the mother ceases, the ovum becomes detached, and finally, probably at some multiple of four weeks, uterine action commences, the mouth and neck of the womb dilate, and the now useless foreign body is expelled.

A totally different category of miscarriages is furnished by the cases in which the ovum is killed owing to a malposition of the womb. Retroversion and retroflection of the womb are not uncommon conditions, but it is only in rare cases that the displacement is so great as to interfere with the continuance of pregnancy. The accident, however, does occur, and will be considered further on so far as its effects on the mother are concerned.

A fourth class of miscarriages is caused by accidental violence. The delicate connection between the ovum and the uterus may be severed by blows, kicks, falls, and similar accidents. In these cases the embryo, the placenta, and the membranes may have been in perfect health up to the time of the disaster, and the embryo may be expelled alive and healthy, although too young to be capable of independent life.

Symptoms of miscarriage.—It will be well

to think of the symptoms of miscarriage as they occur during the first three months, and as they occur from the end of that time up to the end of the seventh month, and to reserve premature birth for separate consideration.

Up to *the end of the third month* the connection between the ovum and the uterus is comparatively fragile. The ovum at this time consists of the embryo enclosed in a little bag of membranes, clear and transparent, except at one part where it is attached to the wall of the uterus by means of very numerous fine threads called *villi*. These villi may be compared to the primitive rootlets of plants; like them, they are fine, almost hair-like, they grow into the mucous membrane of the womb as the rootlet grows into the soil, and, again, like the rootlet, they obtain from their soil the nourishment that is necessary for the new creature. These villi, minute as they are, contain bloodvessels, some going from the ovum to the mother, others from the mother to the ovum, thus establishing a mutual circulation. From somewhere about the centre of this patch of villi a little cord proceeds, attached at the other end to the abdomen of the fœtus. The cord is known as the *funis* or *umbilical cord*, and the point on the abdomen at which the vessels enter and leave is known as the *navel* or *umbilicus*.

After the end of the third month the con-

Abnormal Pregnancy

nection between mother and child becomes much more complicated and much stronger. The villi with their contained vessels branch and re-branch in every direction, thrusting themselves vertically and laterally into the enormously thickened and developed mucous membrane of the uterus. Thus is formed the *placenta* or *afterbirth*, a structure so intimately interwoven with the substance of the uterus that its mechanical detachment is unlikely to occur until certain subtle changes have happened prepara-tory to its natural separation when full term has come ; then the whole ovum is ready to be shed just as a ripe fruit is ready to fall from the tree.

It is quite evident, then, that until after the end of the third month relatively slight acci-dents may suffice to cause miscarriage. Some of the delicate villi may be ruptured and a little blood is effused, which tends to separate a por-tion of the ovum from the wall of the womb. That portion of the ovum is thus rendered more or less a " foreign body," and at the same time the uterus is stimulated to action, and so we have immediately the two great elements of miscarriage with one cause—hæmorrhage, pro-ducing both separation of the ovum and uterine contraction.

The signs and symptoms of early miscarriage are extremely simple. It has been remarked that before a miscarriage occurs the woman often feels an unusual lassitude and disinclination for exertion, but the first definite symptom that arouses her attention is usually bleeding. This hæmorrhage may be so moderate in amount as to cause no anxiety. During the first two months the patient probably thinks that her hopes of pregnancy were mistaken, and that an ordinary monthly period is commencing. The discharge at first may be brownish-red, or merely mucus stained with blood; it, however, increases in quantity, and after a time is accompanied by pain. This pain may be at first similar to the monthly backache from which some women suffer, but unless the process is arrested the pain soon becomes definitely paroxysmal in character and resembles the pains in the first stage of labour. Sometimes the pain of miscarriage is very severe. The uterus is not ready to expel its contents; the neck and mouth of the womb are not softened and prepared as they are at full term, but stiff and rigid, and the dilating process is very painful. However, all the pain occurs during the first stage of the miniature labour; the second stage—i.e. the expulsion of the ovum—is easy and painless in proportion to its small size and ready compressibility.

Up to the end of the third month the ovum is frequently expelled entire, and if the miscarriage be the result of accident the miniature child can be seen floating in its clear water, the *liquor amnii*, possibly making feeble movements with its tiny limbs. Of course, these almost immediately cease.

The treatment of such a miscarriage is usually limited to an attempt to stop its progress. If a doctor be consulted, or if the patient suspect the truth, very naturally she will go to bed and stay there. The quieter she keeps, and the less fuss and disturbance of mind and body, the better the chance of averting miscarriage. Unfortunately, in the great majority of cases the warning hæmorrhage is quickly succeeded by pain, and when these two symptoms are established the threatened miscarriage usually occurs.

An attempt may be made to stop hæmorrhage and uterine action by the administration of 15 grains of bromide of potassium by the mouth and a starch and opium enema by the bowel (Appendix, Formula 4). Food should be restricted to liquids, and these should not be taken hot. The patient should retain the recumbent position, and should not rise to answer the calls of Nature.

In the few instances in which the hæmorrhage is sufficient to cause pallor or to quicken the pulse, ergot may be given (a small teaspoonful of the ammoniated tincture in a wineglass of water), and if a doctor be present the vagina may be plugged. The material used for the plug should be sterilised gauze, preferably bismuth gauze or iodoform gauze. Gauze impregnated with corrosive sublimate or other dangerous chemicals should not be employed. The nurse, if one be in attendance, should first thoroughly wash the vulva and adjacent parts, and should administer a douche (a quart or two of water, temperature about 105° F., containing to each quart two teaspoonfuls of tincture of iodine, a tablespoonful of Sanitas, or enough Condy's fluid to make the water a good full pink). The gauze packing will probably arrest hæmorrhage and stimulate uterine action, so that after a few hours pain will suddenly cease, and on withdrawal of the pack the ovum will be found lying on the top.

Miscarriage during *the middle portion of pregnancy* is more often caused by disease, and is therefore a more serious process. It occurs when the union between the uterus and the ovum has become more complicated and intimate, and therefore it is a more painful process. Miscarriage at this time also differs from early miscarriage in that it is more often "incomplete"—that is to say, although the embryo and the liquor amnii come away, the membranes and placenta are often retained.

It is quite easy to understand why this should be. The ovum increases in size as pregnancy advances. It contains relatively more fluid, and its union with the mucous membrane of the womb is much closer, much tougher, and much more difficult to separate. The contractions of the womb, therefore, are of necessity much stronger, and the neck and mouth of the womb yield with difficulty; consequently, the ovum is burst open, and first the water and then the embryo are easily expelled, but the expulsion of the placenta and membranes presents more difficulty. In these cases the whole process is more prolonged, there are more hæmorrhage and more pain, and therefore more exhaustion. The whole affair is abnormal; it has probably commenced in disease; both the uterus and its contents are unhealthy, and the consequences to the mother are much more serious than is usually the case when abortion occurs in the earlier weeks. Owing to this tendency to incompleteness, many cases of miscarriage during the middle term of pregnancy need skilful management; they require packing, and in some instances the retained portions of the ovum have to be removed under anæsthesia.

It may happen that neither doctor nor midwife is in attendance from the beginning of the process; also it is very likely that a diseased embryo, quite unrecognisable to the ordinary eye, may have been passed enveloped in one of the many bloodclots. It is absolutely essential, therefore, that everything that is passed during miscarriage should be put aside for careful inspection by the medical attendant. All clots, etc., should be put into a bowl or chamber containing a reliable disinfectant. The doctor will probably have to break up the clots in the search for the embryo, and should putrefaction have commenced, infection of the attendant's hand may ensue. Of course, the doctor should wear indiarubber gloves, but perfection is not always attainable.

It must be carefully remembered by all in attendance on a case of miscarriage, and also by the patient herself, that so long as any portion of the ovum or any bloodclot is retained in the uterus there is a danger both of secondary hæmorrhage and of blood-poisoning. Symptoms that the miscarriage has not been complete must be carefully watched for, and any rise of temperature, any quickening of the pulse, any discharge, especially if it be unpleasant in odour, and any tenderness of the abdomen are sufficient reasons for careful evacuation of the uterus under anæsthesia.

Premature birth.—The expulsion of the contents of the uterus between the end of the twenty-eighth week of pregnancy (when the child is supposed to be viable—that is, capable of an independent existence) up to full term is known as *premature confinement.* The phenomena of premature labour vary from a close approximation to a late miscarriage up to the normal course of labour at full term. Premature birth occurring during the eighth month will probably have the initial hæmorrhage, the severe pain, the slow, unsatisfactory first stage, and the short second stage which characterise miscarriage. Every additional week, however, will bring the labour nearer and nearer to the natural standard.

Premature labour is, however, an accident which gives rise to considerable anxiety both for the mother and the child. To begin with, it is very frequently the consequence of disease, and, so far as the infant is concerned, the combination of disease and prematurity generally means death. In another class of cases, however, premature labour is caused by some disease of, or accident to, the mother. It may be the result of one of the toxic diseases, such as *albuminuria* or *eclampsia*, or it may be due to severe hæmorrhage, the result of a premature detachment of the placenta. In any such case the mother's life, as well as that of the infant, is in very great danger, not so much from the prematurity of the labour as from its exciting cause.

In all these anxious cases the doctor should be summoned as quickly as possible. The only hope for both mother and child depends on the promptitude and skill with which the emergency is faced. When skilled medical attention is procurable it is quite fair to assure the mother that she need not be anxious about herself, but no promises should be made with regard to the life of the child.

In spite of all the dangers and anxieties, it may happen that the child survives its birth, even in cases where the prematurity is the result of accident or disease. Of course, in cases in which labour has been induced on account of disproportion between the size of the child and the pelvis, and in some cases where the ill health of the mother makes such a procedure desirable, it is hoped that the induction will save the child's life, and in the great majority of instances the effort is successful.

Care of the premature infant.—The infant is feeble and delicate in proportion to its immaturity, and requires great and unremitting care for the first year or so after birth. The degree of care required and the hope of successful rearing depend chiefly on the time at which labour occurred. Thus, it is evident that the child that has enjoyed the hospitality of its mother's womb up to the thirty-sixth week is probably better nourished and better developed than the child that was born at the end of the seventh month. Immaturity, however, is at least as potent a factor in the fate of the child as is prematurity, and therefore some infants have a better chance at thirty-two weeks than others have at thirty-six.

In all cases where labour is premature the greatest consideration must be shown to the child throughout its course. The mother's strength, too, must be jealously guarded. She must be kept warm and at perfect rest, and the labour must, if necessary, be accelerated. The new-born infant must be immediately wrapped in cotton wool and laid in a specially prepared and well-warmed cradle. In hospitals and other public institutions special incubators are available for all delicate and premature infants, but there is no difficulty in improvising a sufficiently good incubator in the home. An ordinary cradle or a suitable box should have its sides thoroughly padded with many layers of cotton wool, and over this a soft new blanket or thick woollen shawl should be placed. Two or three hot-water bottles should be put between the blanket and the cotton wool. In the case of the box it will suffice to fill four quart bottles with water just below boiling-point and place them one at each corner of the box in an upright position. The cradle should be surrounded on three sides by a screen which is not too high, and over it a rug or thick shawl should be draped to form a tent in order to ward off draughts. The baby should not be dressed, but, having been rapidly oiled, should be swathed in cotton wool and immediately put into its nest. Careful provision should be made for the reception and removal of the excreta, but in many instances it will be better not to give the child a general bath, nor to dress it, for three weeks or a month.

The feeding of the premature child presents considerable difficulty. It is quite likely that the mother's condition may retard the secretion of milk, and even should she fortunately have sufficient milk, the infant may be too feeble to be able to suck. In cases where the mother has no milk an attempt must be made to feed the child with peptonised milk, Glaxo, Albulactin, or whipped white of egg. In cases of extreme feebleness it may be necessary to add two or three drops of brandy to some of the feeds. If it is possible to get the child to suck, the effort to do so must be made ; the food is much better digested when taken in that fashion, but it is sometimes necessary to use an eggspoon, and then great care must be taken not to give too much at a time and not to feed the child too often. An enormous amount of care, patience, and resource is necessary in dealing with some of these difficult cases, but the reward is great if the little one can be persuaded to live.

In the case of those infants who are extremely feeble or obviously diseased, the chief effort must be directed to the mother, and to consoling her for the disappointment of her hopes.

CHAPTER IV

DISEASES OF PREGNANCY: TOXIC, NERVOUS, AND MECHANICAL

Toxic Diseases

PREGNANCY is a normal condition and not a disease. All the same, the strain on every part of the organism is so great that the normal constantly approaches the abnormal, the functions of the different organs of the body need careful supervision, and, in order to maintain health, watchfulness and common sense are essential.

In writing of the signs and symptoms of pregnancy morning sickness was mentioned, and it was indicated that this uncomfortable condition was, as a rule, not a sign of disease. In some unfortunate cases the sickness, instead of being limited to the morning, and instead of existing during a few weeks only, may be urgent, distressing, constant throughout the day, and it may occasionally last up to the very end of pregnancy. This "pernicious vomiting of pregnancy," as it is called, may belong to the *nervous* or to the *toxic* class of disease. When nervous, the sickness, although distressing—and it may be very frequent—does not appear to cause a very serious disturbance of health. The patient may be utterly miserable and very much worried ; she says that she retains no food, and that she gets little or no sleep ; at the same time, she does not lose weight to any great extent, and her complexion, although it may be pale, is not of the yellow-grey tint which usually accompanies poisoning. Such a woman is often very impatient, and urgently desires that her pregnancy should end. Careful inquiry will frequently elicit the fact that she is suffering from business or family worries, or perhaps she is very nervous about herself and anxious about the result of her pregnancy. In such a case much can be done to restore the nervous balance and to help the woman to go on with better cheer until the pregnancy comes to a natural and satisfactory conclusion. The doctor will probably order some soothing drug, such as 15 grains of bromide of potassium, to be taken every six or eight hours for a few days. Possibly other drugs may be advised. The domestic management, which is quite as important as the medical, consists in keeping the patient absolutely at rest in bed, isolated from all friends, the only visitors admitted to her chamber being her husband and mother if they are discreet and cheerful. No one likely to bring worries or anxieties can be allowed. Every effort must be made to calm and cheer the patient's mind and to stimulate her hopes of a happy conclusion to her troubles.

In really severe cases ordinary meals should be stopped, and nourishment, such as peptonised milk, junket, Benger's Food, Brand's Essence, and meat juice suitably diluted, should be given in teaspoonful doses every ten minutes. The food may be cooled with ice, but must not be icy cold, and its effect must be carefully watched. If it is retained, the quantity administered may be gradually increased, and so, too, may be the intervals between the feeds. In the majority of nervous cases this treatment will be quickly successful, and after a few days the patient may be gradually permitted to resume her ordinary life ; but great care will be needed up to the middle of pregnancy to avoid excitement, over-fatigue, and worry.

The serious cases are those that are dependent not on one of the remediable causes of vomiting, but on a real poisoning of the system. In the beginning it may be difficult to differentiate between the toxic and the nervous forms, but in the former the temperature is likely to rise, so, too, is the pulse-rate. The vomiting is not only frequent and prolonged, but peculiarly distressing in character. The tongue and mouth are dry, the abdomen is tender, and the bowels are usually much constipated. Strength, colour, and flesh are lost with great rapidity, and in many cases there is a true insomnia. Before the symptoms become pronounced there is always a hope that the trouble may be of the type that is amenable to treatment, but if after a few days there is deterioration rather than improvement, the only hope of saving the woman's life lies in the evacuation of the uterus.

Artificial abortion is an operation from which every conscientious doctor recoils. Should it become necessary, the consent of the patient's husband should be obtained in writing, and the operation should not be done until after careful consultation with a reliable colleague. It is a very grave responsibility, involving the destruction of a human life. If the operation be done too soon, the practitioner cannot but feel that it might perhaps have been avoided ; if, however, it is done too late, it will have been done in vain, and the futile attempt to save the embryo will have cost the mother her life.

Closely allied to this form of toxæmia is a peculiar form of jaundice rarely seen except during a first pregnancy. The skin becomes yellow, the motions are light in colour, and the urine dark. All the symptoms of toxic disease are present, and in addition the liver is found to waste very rapidly ; when the doctor percusses it, instead of the dull sound extending to the edge of the ribs, as is natural, it falls far short of that landmark. This so-called **acute yellow**

atrophy of the liver is, so far as is known at present, incurable ; the only hope is to prevent the development of the poison by careful attention to the habits and functions of all pregnant women.

A third manifestation of toxic disease is to be found in **convulsions,** so-called **eclampsia.** This trouble is generally found in connection with albuminuria, and it is to watch against the commencement of kidney disease that the urine of pregnant women ought to be examined at least once a month. The early symptoms of albuminuria may not attract the patient's attention ; a little headache, a transient giddiness or drowsiness, accompanied by a very moderate amount of puffiness of the ankles, would probably escape attention, and the disease would progress, until apparently sudden dropsy, with marked headache, dimness of vision, and one or more fits of convulsions, would announce not only the existence of the disease but its great gravity. In all these toxic diseases *prevention* is the right treatment, for once they are fully developed, cure is difficult and, to say the least, uncertain.

NERVOUS DISEASES

The nervous constitution of a pregnant woman has been aptly likened to the condition of a Leyden jar, for just as the Leyden jar is in a highly unstable electrical condition and is very easily discharged, so is the woman's nervous system unstable, and she is liable to many different varieties of nerve storm. The most serious of these storms—that is, undue vomiting—has been already described; but in addition to this she may have very tiresome *salivation*. The saliva may flow away in large amount, sometimes as much as two quarts in the twenty-four hours. The condition is without danger, but not without inconvenience.

Nervous **headache** may give rise to considerable trouble, and the nervous element may be reinforced by unsuspected errors of refraction. This over sight or short sight ought to have been detected and corrected in childhood. Sometimes the condition escapes recognition, and it is certainly worth while for anyone suffering from headache to pay a visit to the oculist.

Neuralgia, too, may occur in the head or in the jaw; but just as neuralgia in the head may be aggravated by errors of refraction, so neuralgia in the face and jaw is often due to decayed teeth. It is really incomprehensible how people of common sense and refinement can tolerate the presence of decayed teeth in their mouths. In these cases the dentist is the necessary friend, and all palliatives, of which there are only too many, ought to be avoided, because they are only putting off the inevitable and most desirable removal of the offending tooth. Many women

hold the superstition that it is dangerous to have
a tooth extracted during pregnancy. This belief
has absolutely no foundation in fact ; and if the
extraction is done—as it should be—under anæsthesia, the patient will not experience the slightest
shock or inconvenience.

Disorders of the circulation.—In consequence of the greatly increased work demanded
of the heart, it is natural that during pregnancy
it should increase both in size and in vigour.
Throughout the nine months there is a constantly
increasing strain. The heart has to pump the
blood not only throughout the mother's system,
as in the non-pregnant state, but also through
the constantly growing uterus, the placenta, and
the child. It is easy to understand that in
order to do this work satisfactorily the heart
also must increase in size and in vigour of action.
In cases where the heart is sound to start with
and no special strain is involved by the woman's
method of life, the necessary hypertrophy occurs
in absolute physiological proportion, and no discomfort occurs ; but in cases where the heart
has been already damaged by rheumatic fever
or any similar cause, or where the muscles of
the heart are weak and flabby, there is sure to
be discomfort, and sometimes real injury. The
commonest symptom to attract attention is
breathlessness (dyspnœa) ; the patient is uncomfortable when she is called upon to make any

extra exertion, such as walking up hill or running upstairs. Usually the trouble amounts to discomfort only, but in more serious cases palpitation, faintness, and pallor or blueness of the face occur. Cases such as these are generally complicated by anæmia, and, indeed, anæmia is capable of producing such symptoms even when the heart is absolutely normal.

The patient should avoid sudden exertion and muscular strain. Steady, quiet exercise will do good, but she must not lift heavy weights or pull out drawers full of, say, linen or books, and she should avoid everything that entails her working with her arms raised above her head. The circulation should be relieved by careful attention to the bowels (see p. 159). The digestion should be helped by taking food easy of digestion and not excessive in quantity. Heart distress is always made worse when the stomach and bowels are over-distended. For the immediate treatment of cardiac distress, rest in a comfortable easy chair is usually more effectual than lying down. A teaspoonful of sal volatile in half a tumblerful of hot water, or an equal quantity of spirit of red lavender, will be found very helpful. It is also important for the patient to remember that a certain amount of distress may occur without there being any worse mischief than indigestion.

For palpitation the same remedies may be

Diseases of Pregnancy

tried, and the clothes should be loosened. Women are, perhaps, more alarmed by attacks of faintness than by breathlessness and palpitation ; or, if they are not, their friends are likely to be so. The causes are probably the same in all three cases, and it will be found that faintness is apt to occur after a hastily eaten meal, or sudden, and under the circumstances undue, exertion. A most important point in the treatment of faintness is to place the head lower than the heart. In the non-pregnant condition this is readily achieved by sitting down and bending forward until the head rests on the knees, but such a position is obviously inappropriate during pregnancy. The pregnant woman should lie down without any pillows under her head, her hips and legs being well raised. Smelling salts and eau-de-Cologne or lavender water will be found very serviceable, also a dose of sal volatile in hot water, or some similar stimulant. The patient should be thoroughly reassured as to her condition, because for one case in which fainting indicates real disease there are hundreds in which it depends on flatulence, a hasty meal, or over-exertion.

Varicose veins.—The blood-vessels share in the increased growth (hypertrophy) of the heart common in pregnancy. In addition to this hypertrophy, the growing womb leads to a constantly increasing pressure on the veins of the lower extremities. In consequence, there is a difficulty in the return of the venous blood. The valves of the veins become over-strained and sometimes cease to be effectual; the vessels then are overfilled and dilated as well as hypertrophied. The more superficial of them, immediately below the skin, become tortuous, and present the well-known characters of varicose veins; that is to say, they are unduly prominent, large, and blue, and can be felt through the skin like bunches of fat earthworms. The patient suffers from a feeling of weight and tension in the legs, sometimes amounting to great discomfort. This is generally accompanied by a certain amount of œdema or swelling, and occasionally the skin of the part is reddened and irritable. It is quite rare for the varicose veins of pregnancy to ulcerate, but it is possible that, in the case of a woman who has had eczema of the legs a sore may form which, if neglected, may lead to ulceration. From such an ulcer there may be much hæmorrhage, which will certainly not be controlled by bathing or dabbing; it will be necessary to put on a graduated compress and to bandage the limb from the roots of the toes upwards with an elastic, a crêpe velpeau, or an open-wove bandage 3 inches wide. Such a bandage both affords sufficient support and makes the pressure at the bleeding-point effectual.

Hæmorrhoids or piles.—A special form of

Diseases of Pregnancy

varicose vein, which is very common and distressing during pregnancy, occurs about the opening of the bowel. Piles are essentially varicose veins in which, frequently, the blood has clotted, and the bunch of veins is surrounded by loose and overgrown tissue just within, and perhaps just without, the anal margin. Owing to its position, and to the great difficulty of maintaining local cleanliness, such hæmorrhoids are very likely to become inflamed and to lose their superficial covering. In this case the patient's distress is aggravated both by the symptoms of inflammation—swelling, heat, and pain—and also by a discharge of blood or blood-stained matter. The amount of blood lost is seldom important, but the annoyance caused by the discharge is very great.

The tendency to piles, which is inevitable in pregnancy, is greatly aggravated in women of sedentary habit, and even more in women who habitually neglect their bowels. Congestion of the mucous membrane of the anus is at all times readily caused by pressure of hard masses in the lower bowel, and when to this is added the pressure of the enlarging womb the existence of piles during pregnancy is easy to understand.

Strict attention to diet, omitting all alcohol, salted meats, and highly spiced foods, is of the first importance, and so is intelligent care of the bowels. This point will be considered later, under the heading of CONSTIPATION, but the piles themselves must receive some palliative attention. Hamamelis suppositories may be introduced, one every night, or one after the daily evacuation of the bowel. It is necessary that the patient should lie down after the insertion of the suppository, or it probably will be rapidly pushed out. It is to be remembered that the suppository is really a little cone of ointment, sufficiently stiff to admit of its introduction, and that the same materials that are useful in the form of a suppository are also effectual for the treatment of external piles when applied in the form of an ointment (Appendix, Formula 5).

Sometimes, but very rarely, it will happen that palliative treatment does not suffice for the effectual relief of the symptoms of piles. In such cases the medical attendant may think it wise to remove them. This proposal should not alarm the patient, for when carefully performed no trouble, and certainly no miscarriage, is likely to follow.

Occasionally varicose veins form about the vulva and within the vagina. The symptoms are very similar to those caused by piles; the doctor, if one is available, should in all cases be consulted, but where this is impossible considerable relief may be obtained by attention to the rules laid down for the treatment of piles and by maintenance of the recumbent position.

Diseases of Pregnancy

Constipation. — This condition during pregnancy arises from mechanical causes, diversion of nervous energy, and errors in diet. The pressure of the growing womb affects the bowel directly by diminishing its lumen (channel). The nervous energy is largely diverted to the womb and its contents, while as to errors of diet and digestion, they appear to be one of the penalties of an irregularly developed civilisation. The more people work with their brains and the less they use their bodies, the more prone are they to suffer from constipation. Also, the more meat eaten in proportion to the bulkier vegetables and fruits, the less the mechanical stimulation of the bowel. And lastly, the tendency to sluggishness of the bowels is increased by the avoidance of all diet that is rough and tough. In addition to all these ordinary causes of constipation, it is necessary to remember that many people do not drink anything like enough watery fluid. A good rule to remember is that an adult should drink about three pints of watery fluid in the day, and should pass on an average the same amount of urine. If too little fluid is drunk the motions tend to be hard and small, and therefore are propelled along the bowel less readily and with more discomfort.

The evils of constipation are very great. When all the useful part of the food has been absorbed, the residue, especially when small or dry, is apt to be retained too long in the lower bowel. Injurious substances are absorbed from it, and the delicate mucous membrane of the large bowel thereby irritated.

Anyone suffering from constipation is likely to have a dirty tongue and unpleasant breath, appetite fails, and the stomach and bowels become more or less distended by flatulence. There are very uneasy feelings, accompanied by rumblings in the abdomen; and sometimes this flatulent distension, in addition to the irritation of the hard masses, leads to the violent spasms of the bowels known as colic. By increasing local pressure, constipation leads to varicose veins and piles, and, paradoxical as it may seem, it is one of the commonest causes of diarrhœa. The retained lumps irritate the delicate mucous membrane and cause it to pour out an excess of fluid and mucus. This secretion, tinged with a little fæcal matter, is expelled from the bowel, probably two or three times in rapid succession, and the patient, not recognising the cause of her trouble, is apt to take chlorodyne, or chalk mixture, both of which remedies only make bad worse, whereas a dose of castor oil, by sweeping away the offending material, would quickly give relief. Castor oil, however, must not be regarded as a remedy for constipation. It is an excellent agent for securing a thorough evacuation of the intestinal canal, but, as a rule, it does its work

Diseases of Pregnancy

so thoroughly that no action ensues for the next two or three days.

In the first instance, constipation should be treated by diet and general good management. Plenty of cereals, vegetables, and fruit should be eaten, also other foods which are unirritating and leave a fairly bulky residuum, such, for instance, as suet puddings of various sorts. Contrary to the usual belief, milk is not constipating to the ordinary individual, and the faeces resulting from it are fairly voluminous. Much good may also be done by taking a glass of water night and morning, or a large glass of lemonade at bedtime sweetened with glycerin (a tablespoonful of lemon juice and a dessertspoonful of glycerin to half a pint of hot water).

Attention should be paid to exercise, which should be steady and abundant but never sudden or irregular. Probably walking and motoring in moderation will be most useful, and, for those who are accustomed to such exercise, bicycling and horse-riding may be continued so long as they are not too inconvenient.

With regard to drugs, the more they are avoided the better. But the evils which arise from our artificial mode of existence frequently necessitate artificial remedies. Among the most useful of aperients is cascara. This drug may be taken in many forms : cascara evacuant, cascara and malt, cascaraloin in tabloids, and ordinary cascara tabloids, sugar-coated, of one, two, or three grains each. Preparations of senna, such as syrup of figs and infusion of senna pods, also compound liquorice powder, of which this drug is the basis, are effectual, and seldom cause griping. There are innumerable good pills, tabloids, and dragées on the market, and it will be found necessary to vary the aperient constantly; indeed, it is a good plan to have a list of seven to ten and to take them in rotation.

Although aperients should be avoided as far as possible, it is wiser to take a small dose every night than to take a large one after a longer interval, when the constipation has become formidable.

Massage is an excellent remedy for constipation, but its application must be extremely limited during gestation. A safer remedy will be found in an abdominal pack. A well-fitting belt can be made covered with waterproof jaconet; on the inner surface three slots made of tape should be sewn (one in the centre and one at each side about 3 inches distant from it), a large folded handkerchief or a piece of lint, some 8 inches in depth and 12 to 15 inches in length, should be wrung out of warm water and passed under the slots. This belt is secured round the body by straps and buckles or some similar contrivance, and it is prevented from riding up by a T bandage or sanitary towel

Diseases of Pregnancy

fastened to the belt before and behind. This simple contrivance, by assisting and equalising the circulation in the abdomen, and also by its stimulating influence on the nerves of the skin and the intestines, not only assists the action of the bowels, but is also useful in procuring sleep.

Enemata are useful in the treatment of constipation. As a rule, an enema of simple warm water, about a pint or a pint and a half, will be found helpful, but in cases of obstinate constipation an oil enema (Appendix, Formula 8) or a magnesium sulphate enema (Appendix, Formula 6) will be efficient. One great objection to an enema is that it is tiresome for self-administration, and unless nicely done the introduction of the nozzle of the siphon syringe may injure, or at any rate bruise, the anus. Some women find great relief from the use of a glycerin enema ; quite a small quantity of glycerin is used by means of a small special syringe, which can be bought of any chemist, or aperient suppositories of glycerin or cacao butter may be used. Aperient suppositories, unlike the ordinary medicated ones, should be introduced on first rising in the morning, and may be expected to act before breakfast.

· **Diarrhoea.** — This trouble is most frequently caused by constipation, as mentioned above, but it may also be the result of irritating articles of diet, and is a prominent symptom in the grave condition known as ptomaine poisoning which follows the consumption of decaying and mouldy articles of diet. When diarrhœa can be traced to any such cause the obvious treatment is to get rid of the poison by the administration of castor oil. The accompanying weakness, nausea, and faintness should be met by rest in bed, the use of a woollen nightgown and binder, the application of hot bottles to the stomach and feet, and the administration of a small quantity of hot brandy and water; a dessertspoonful of the spirit will suffice. Ptomaine poisoning is frequently of so serious a nature as to need immediate medical attention, but it is also an accident of such urgency that the simple treatment sketched above should be used until the doctor arrives.

Another cause of diarrhœa in pregnancy is simple indigestion, the stomach and bowels being irritated by a mass of unripe fruit, by pips, skins, and caraway seeds, hard peas, and stringy beans. Prevention is the best cure, but for the immediate relief of suffering an emetic, followed by evacuation of the bowels, will suffice.

It is extraordinary how unwise is the general domestic treatment of these so-called bilious attacks. The stomach, having been overloaded, or having contended in vain with indigestible food, succeeds after a long struggle in ejecting the offender. Peace should now be restored, but

Diseases of Pregnancy

anxious friends, though never the patient, are immediately desirous of cramming the unfortunate organ with more food. The one thing that the stomach needs is a few hours' rest, assisted by a drink of warm water to wash it out.

All forms of diarrhœa may be aggravated by fatigue and chill, but this additional cause does not need any different treatment from that described. After a few hours of rest and so-called starvation, the, patient may gradually return to the simple diet that is appropriate to her pregnant condition.

So much for the simple every-day forms of diarrhœa. It is, however, to be remembered that loose or watery stools frequently repeated may be a symptom of graver disorders—e.g. of enteric fever, tuberculosis of the intestines, and some forms of blood poisoning. In all cases where the ordinary domestic remedies fail to afford speedy relief medical advice must be sought.

MECHANICAL DISORDERS

Any description of the disorders of pregnancy is liable to the drawback known as cross-classification. Thus, neuralgia of the face may be classified as nervous, digestive, or circulatory, according as it is believed that the pain is mainly neurotic, due to carious teeth, or dependent on a vitiation or deficiency of the blood. So, too, with the mechanical disorders of pregnancy. Undoubtedly these ought to include such pressure effects as piles and varicose veins, but for convenience of description this heading is reserved for the effects on gestation of those displacements of the pregnant uterus which are termed retroflexion and retroversion.

A uterus which is displaced backwards may become pregnant, and as a general rule no trouble ensues. The organ grows mainly upwards and forwards, so that, like a normally placed womb, it rises into the abdomen. The cases are few and far between in which this normal change of position fails, but very occasionally the whole, or the greater part, of the womb remains in the pelvis and very soon suffers injurious pressure from the bony walls with which it is surrounded. Before long it presses on the rectum, causing constipation or irritation of that organ. It presses, however, with more rapidly injurious effect on the neck of the bladder. In consequence of this pressure the chief symptom of the incarceration of the pregnant uterus is a partial or complete inability to pass water. The patient's distress quickly increases; the more she desires to relieve her bladder, and the more effort she makes, the greater becomes her distress. Fortunately, the condition is easy of recognition. There is a sudden increase in the size of the lower part of the abdomen caused by the distended bladder, and a finger passed into the vagina readily detects a portion of a spherical mass blocking the pelvis.

This condition demands immediate attention, and probably the first thing the doctor will do is to pass a sterilised catheter into the bladder and draw off the urine. The next task is to ascertain whether the uterus can be gently pushed up out of the pelvis. If the condition is recognised early enough, before the womb has become so enlarged or so swollen as to make it unwise to attempt re-position, the treatment is simple; but if, unfortunately, the case has been neglected, it is very probable that the womb may have to be emptied of its contents. The moral is that pregnant women should be very careful to evacuate the bowel and the bladder regularly. An overloaded bladder may prevent the uterus from rising spontaneously into the abdomen, and in any case it greatly aggravates the distress and the danger.

Still more important is the condition of the bladder in those cases in which displacement of the uterus did not exist before pregnancy. If the organ becomes displaced after pregnancy has begun, the chief cause is an overfull bladder pressing the movable uterus downwards and backwards, although this cause may be reinforced by a kick, blow, or fall.

PART IV

THE NURSING MOTHER

CHAPTER I

LACTATION AND WEANING

The secretion of milk. —As stated at p. 89, milk is secreted by the breast long before the birth of the infant, but the amount at that time is usually small, and its secretion is not accompanied by turgescence of the breast or by any constitutional symptoms. The classical phenomena of the commencement of lactation are most frequently seen in the case of a woman in her first confinement (*primipara*). The function is then initiated formally, and with a certain amount of difficulty, but in subsequent confinements the process is usually much easier, and is not accompanied by any noteworthy amount of local discomfort or of general reaction. As a rule, towards the evening of the third day the symptoms begin to be troublesome (*see* p. 126), but after the lapse of thirty-six or forty-eight hours the breast appears to accommodate itself to its new function, the turgescence and pain

168

subside, febrile reaction ceases, and the milk flows freely.

The human breast appears to be, in one sense, a reservoir for the milk, but it is a reservoir the replenishment of which occurs rapidly and at distinct intervals. Most women are perfectly well aware when the fresh " draught of milk " is available. Almost suddenly the breasts, which had been only moderately full, become distended with milk, and in some instances the tension is so great that the fluid runs away spontaneously. Women vary greatly in their capacity for suckling. It has been observed that the daughters of drunkards seldom make good nursing mothers. Whether that is so or not, if a woman is in good health the amount of milk secreted appears to depend largely on the demand made by the baby. A big, vigorous child who sucks strongly is generally rewarded by an abundant meal. The demands of two babies are usually as well met as are the demands of one, provided that the mother is both able and willing to secure for herself an abundance of good food. This fact of the relation of supply to demand is not at all generally recognised by the nursing mother and her friends ; they therefore act on the principle of sparing the breast as far as possible, and in consequence that organ fails to put out its best powers.

Another very common misapprehension is

that the child should at first be put to the breast
every two hours. The " draught of milk " does
not come so often, nor does the healthy infant
either need or desire such frequent suckling. An
infant that is kept dry, warm, and comfortable
may go three, or even four hours between meals ;
it should certainly never be roused in order
that it may be suckled, and the mother will
profit much, locally as well as generally, from
the prolonged rest. It has only recently been
pointed out that the inability of many women
to continue suckling beyond four or five weeks
is really not due to general exhaustion, nor to
the diversion of their energies to household and
other interests, but chiefly to the fact of local
exhaustion, the breast having been required to
supply milk when not physiologically prepared
to do so.

The results of careful experiments made in
various institutions tend to show that infants
increase more rapidly and more steadily in
weight, and that the breast is better able to continue lactation, when the child is fed six, five,
or even so few as four times in twenty-four hours
instead of having the customary eight or ten
meals. More especially is it necessary that the
mother's rest should not be disturbed at night,
and if the rule is observed of changing the child's
napkins sufficiently often and of keeping the
cradle thoroughly well warmed (if necessary

with a hot-water bottle), it will probably sleep from 10 or 11 P.M. to 5 or 6 A.M. from very early days. It is, however, quite hopeless to expect such good behaviour from a child that is uncomfortable in any way. If it be constipated, griped, wet, or dirty, and most assuredly if it be cold, it will wake and cry, and unfortunately the cry of discomfort or pain is frequently mistaken for that of hunger.

Importance of suckling to mother and child. — When the baby is put to the breast and the flow of milk commences, the mother will, for the first few days after confinement, feel what is known as an *after-pain*. These pains depend chiefly on imperfect contraction of the womb, and are less severe after a first confinement than on subsequent occasions. The contraction of the womb is necessary in order that its cavity may be kept healthy and free from the presence of bloodclot. Undoubtedly the proper management of the mother, and especially gentle massage of the abdomen several times a day, will tend to secure this result. So also will the action of suckling. Indirectly it stimulates the uterus, and so assists in the preservation of its tone.

A woman who does not suckle her child usually suffers much from the thwarted function of her breasts. They long remain turgid and painful, her temperature and pulse are unduly liable to variations, and in many instances there is a considerable and prolonged difficulty in stopping the secretion of the milk.

With regard to general health, the nursing mother has a great advantage over the woman who will not suckle. She is able to secure more rest of body ; her appetite, digestion, and general well-being are usually most satisfactory ; she also escapes the inevitable worry and probable anxiety incidental to bringing up a child on the bottle. If the advantages to the mother are great, those accruing to the nursling are greater still. The milk of each mammalian creature is exactly adapted to its own young, and there is no other that can be substituted with equal advantage to the offspring. Not only is cow's milk not thus specially adapted in composition, but the bottle-fed baby is at a very serious disadvantage, because the milk provided for it instead of its mother's milk cannot go direct from producer to consumer, but has to be milked into receptacles much exposed to dirt and dust, and frequently it has to undergo a long journey by train, so that it does not arrive in the nursery until after an interval of many hours. Subtle changes begin in the milk as soon as it is drawn ; these are inevitable, but owing to the singularly careless manner in which milk is treated, the changes are no longer "subtle" by the time the child receives it. Germs of many kinds have time to develop and to multiply ; accidental contamination by dirt has occurred; the milk has been subjected to variations of temperature and thoroughly well shaken; and it is doubtful whether, after all these changes have occurred, this highly putrescible fluid can arrive in a state fit for the nourishment of the delicate organism for which it is destined.

In many instances, too, the method in which milk is administered is unsatisfactory. The storing of milk in most households leaves much to be desired. The jugs or pans in which it is kept are seldom efficiently covered and protected from infection by dust and insects. A few years ago feeding-bottles were very generally so constructed that they could not be thoroughly cleansed, and, worse still, they were furnished with long india-rubber tubes which it was impossible to clean. Thousands of babies died every year from this cause alone, and still more numerous were the cases of infantile cholera, inflammatory diarrhœa, dyspepsia, and failure to thrive. Some improvement has been made quite recently both in the collection and the storage of milk, and a more rational type of feeding-bottle is becoming usual; but any mother who values her own peace of mind and the health of her baby should make not only a determined, but also an intelligent effort to bring it up on its natural food.

Duration of lactation.—There is an old saying that a woman should carry her child nine

173

months and that she should suckle it nine months. As a rough-and-ready rule this is right enough, but the duration of lactation must depend in every case on the health of the mother and of the child. A baby should not be weaned during an acute period of teething, nor during the occurrence of any ailment, neither should it be weaned during a spell of hot weather. The child should in all cases be in good health and under generally favourable circumstances when so serious a revolution is made in its dietary. From the mother's point of view weaning may be rendered desirable by a persistent failure in her health, loss of flesh, and loss of appetite. Probably it is a good thing that even from birth a child should have one meal of pure cow's milk and water once a day. All human beings are liable to illness, and should the mother unfortunately be suddenly incapacitated, it would be good both for herself and her nursling if artificial feeding were not a totally new experience.

If the woman is a good nurse she ought to be able to feed the child herself, with the exception of this one meal, up to the age of six months, but after this time she should nurse the baby about three times in the twenty-four hours and give at any rate two artificial meals a day. A woman's milk alters in character as the child grows older, becoming richer in proteins and in fats, therefore the mixture of milk and water, or milk and barley water, for the child's supplementary meals may gradually be made richer in milk.

How to wean a baby.—In cases where a woman has been able gradually to increase the artificial feeding and withdraw her own milk, weaning practically accomplishes itself. The child's feelings as well as its digestion have been trained to the willing acceptance of the bottle, and although it still prefers the breast there is no sudden shock when this is finally withheld. The case, however, is very different when, owing to the mother's death or sudden incapacity, the process of weaning is abrupt. The child always suffers and sometimes very severely. So far as the woman is concerned, if she is obliged to relinquish her office of nurse—for instance, owing to the child's death—suffering falls on her. The draught of milk continues, the breasts become turgid, but the relief afforded by suckling is no longer available. An attempt should be made to check the secretion by a great reduction in the amount and in the milkiness of her diet. She should also take an efficient dose of a saline purgative, such as Epsom salts, every morning. The breasts should be covered with lint soaked in glycerin of belladonna, and over this there should be a thick layer of cotton wool or gamgee tissue, kept in place with a firm bandage. If the distress is very great a little milk may be drawn from each breast by means of a breast pump, but this should be avoided if possible.

Abnormalities of lactation.—In some women who are otherwise normal and quite healthy there may be a deficiency in the secretion of milk. An effort should be made to remedy this condition by a generous diet of ordinary food plus two or three pints of milk a day. In addition to this she may take some preparation of malt, especially malt with cod-liver oil, if it be winter. There are many drugs and preparations (galactagogues) which stimulate the secretion of milk, such as lacteol and the preparations of pituitrin. It is, however, wiser that a woman should not take drugs without the advice of her medical attendant, and more especially is this the case with such a powerful drug as pituitrin.

In other cases there may be a superabundance of milk, the secretion flowing away to such an extent as to swamp the clothing. Not much can be done to combat this condition, because the drugs that might diminish the flow of milk would also probably injure the nursling. Means should be taken to protect the mother's clothes and to secure her comfort, and it is not likely that the inconvenience will be of long duration.

Abscess of the breast.—Abscess of the breast most frequently occurs in the very early days of suckling, and more especially in the case of a first confinement. It is generally due to infection entering through some minute crack or abrasion. The epithelium covering the nipple and the surrounding areola is extremely thin and delicate, and if means have not been taken to render it tougher and more supple during the later months of pregnancy, some amount of injury is sure to be caused by the baby's efforts. Even ordinary sucking inflicts some injury, but some babies absolutely bite with their gums, especially when over-hungry or annoyed. The cracks and abrasions are inevitable, but much can be done to prevent infection. The baby's mouth and lips should be washed before and after suckling ; the breast should receive similar attention, and after suckling it should be smeared with some antiseptic and soothing ointment (Appendix, Formula 7). If the nipple be specially tender, and the baby's sucking causes a flow of blood, it is well that it should be made to suck through a nipple shield to which an indiarubber nipple is fixed. Great care must be taken that the artificial nipple is cleansed and boiled every time it is used. Also it must be firmly fixed to the glass shield, otherwise the baby may suck it off. In cases where there is much soreness of the nipple a good old-fashioned contrivance, known as Dr. Wansborough's nipple shield, may be worn between each feed. These nipple shields are of soft lead, and when acted on by the milk a mild solution resembling lead lotion is formed.

This makes a very soothing application, but it must be carefully washed away before the infant is put to the breast.

When one or more cracks or sores are visible they may be lightly touched with a stick of mitigated caustic, or the minutest possible drop of carbolic acid. These applications cause a sharp pain, but it is not lasting, and the caustic destroys the micro-organisms which might otherwise produce infection of the breast and so cause abscess.

Sometimes, without any obvious reason, but still more frequently from evident carelessness, infection does occur. This may fortunately be superficial, when the abscess causes relatively little suffering, quickly comes to a head, and either bursts spontaneously or can be cured by a very trifling incision for which gas anæsthesia, or even painting the part with cocaine, will suffice. In such cases lactation need not be interrupted ; a glass shield can be worn during suckling, and after suckling a little cocaine ointment may be applied on gauze or lint (Appendix, Formula 8).

In some instances, however, the infection travels deeper into the substance of the gland, and instead of the slight redness and puffiness that characterise the superficial variety of abscess, a tender lump forms in the substance of the organ. This lump is not only tender but very painful, especially during the " draught of milk " and

Lactation and Weaning

during suckling. The woman's health suffers; she becomes feverish, loses her appetite, endures pain all the day, and is kept awake by it at night. Gradually the lump increases and comes nearer to the surface of the breast; the skin over it reddens and is exquisitely tender; the pain radiates in all directions, especially into the axilla. Such an abscess must be treated by restricted diet, free purgation, constant fomentations, support to the breasts, and rest in bed. The sooner the surgeon's aid is invoked the better, for a free incision under anæsthesia and thorough drainage will put an end to the trouble, and the woman may perhaps be able to resume nursing with the affected breast after a time.

In cases where an abscess is neglected the infection spreads to other parts of the breast and sometimes to the armpit. Multiple abscesses are thus formed, the woman endures a serious illness, and in some instances the power of the injured breast to secrete milk is lost for ever.

CHAPTER II

ARTIFICIAL FEEDING AND WET-NURSING

No effort should be considered too great, and no perseverance too obstinate, to enable a woman to suckle her child. Still, some few cases will always exist where the infant is inevitably deprived of its natural nourishment. It is therefore necessary to consider possible substitutes.

In some respects nursing by another woman would appear to be the obvious solution of the difficulty. It *is* a solution, but it is never satisfactory, and sometimes is disastrous. To begin with, it is an injustice towards the foster mother's own child should it be living. The young woman is taken from her home, her husband, and her children; the baby she abandons in favour of the rich woman's child is very likely to die because it is not only deprived of its natural food and its mother's personal care, but its circumstances are such that it is extremely difficult for it to obtain pure milk and adequate attention. It is a very serious responsibility for any young woman to undertake, and the evil entailed does not affect the poor child only. The foster mother is probably worried and anxious about her neglected home and abandoned baby, and her anxiety is likely to affect her health and to depreciate the quantity and quality of her milk.

Another very real danger is that even where a doctor's opinion can be had as to the physical soundness of the foster mother and the probability of her being able to supply milk sufficient in quantity and good in quality, it is impossible to be certain that she is healthy in herself and comes of a healthy stock. A very careful medical examination should always be made, not only of the young woman but of her husband and her child. Any evidence of the existence of constitutional disease in any one of the three should lead to rejection. Without going into detail, it is of the first importance that the foster mother's own child should be at least of average size and weight for its age, that its eyes and hair should be bright, the skin of its whole body healthy, with no sores or scars of sores round its mouth and anus, and also that it should be fat and muscular, and entirely free from all suspicion of a snuffling cold in the head.

It is possible, too, that a foster mother may be physically sound and desirable, and yet faults of habit, disposition, and temper may make her absolutely unfit for the office she seeks. Her position in the household is a difficult one : her intimate relation to the nursling and the care that is necessary in her diet and general surroundings bring her much in contact with the family; at the same time she is really of the servant class, and her sympathies will probably be with them. As a rule, either undue gossiping and waste of time with her fellow-servants leads to neglect of the baby, or their jealousy is excited and their consequent unkindness makes the wet-nurse unhappy, and so her efficiency is marred.

In arranging for the welfare of a wet-nurse all these considerations must be borne in mind, and her food, although good in quality and sufficient in quantity, should never be luxurious. She should have plenty of exercise without undue fatigue, and should, so far as is possible, have the care of her nursling and assist in the ordinary nursery duties.

Comparison of various milks.—Where no human milk is available for the baby, it is necessary to decide which of the domestic animals affords the most suitable substitute. Cow's milk immediately suggests itself, for it is generally available and not too expensive. The composition of cow's milk, however, differs very considerably from that of the woman. It contains altogether more solids, and is especially rich in the proteins or flesh-forming elements. If this were the only difference, simple dilution would suffice; but cow's milk contains rather less butter and sugar than does the human, therefore both cream and milk sugar must be added (Appendix, Formula 9). There is another and subtler difference, in that the clot or curd of cow's milk is denser and more difficult of digestion than is that of human milk. This difference is not mitigated by dilution, and in some instances the curd of cow's milk proves altogether too solid for the baby's digestion. The milk then has to be to some extent pre-digested by the action of pepsin.

Ass's milk closely resembles human milk in composition and in digestibility, but unfortunately it is by no means easy to procure, especially in towns.

Goat's milk is rarely used in England, but it is a refuge for the destitute on board ship, in India, and some other places abroad. Before resolving to feed a child on goat's milk, it is necessary to ascertain that the animal from which it is derived is not capable of infecting the infant with so-called Malta or Mediterranean fever. The milk furnished by the goat is richer both in proteins and in fats than is human milk, and therefore needs suitable dilution. It has also an odour and flavour that adults disguise by the addition of tea or coffee, but which is seldom objected to by the baby.

Sterilisation and pasteurisation of milk. —A suitable milk having been selected for the infant, the next difficulty to arise is the certainty that so highly putrescible a fluid can scarcely be kept untainted up to the moment of its use by the child. The sterilisation of nursery milk should be undertaken in the first instance by the dairy farmer, and it should be packed in properly secured and sealed bottles. Naturally, such extra care would entail an increase of price, but neither the private consumer nor the State should hesitate in securing for the children of the nation so real an advantage.

Up to the present time, sterilisation and pasteurisation of milk has been done chiefly in the house of the consumer. (Appendix, Formula 10.) Reference may here be made to the excellent Walker Gordon Laboratory, which supplies milk of any required composition and richness.

Quantity and quality of meals. — Careful rules have been laid down as to the quantity of food to be offered to an infant at each feed, and there has been a general consensus of opinion that the capacity of the infant's stomach at birth is approximately 1 oz. It is probably true that this is the capacity of the stomach when measured *post mortem*, but it is certain that in the case of the living child the capacity to take food varies greatly. A vigorous child weighing 8 lb. or 10 lb. must surely be able to take a much larger meal than a delicate infant weighing only 5 lb. or 6 lb. Also, apart from size, infants, like adults, have varying appetites and desires for food.

It has recently been suggested that, in addition to a variation in size of the stomach, there may be a variation in the capacity for rapid absorption of the water of the milk, which is at least 95 per cent. of the bulk. In any case, it is certain, from weighing-experiments, that while few infants take less than the regulation ounce, most of them exceed the allowance if permitted to do so. So long as an infant sucks uninterruptedly, either from the breast or from a bottle with a suitable teat, there is no fear of its overburdening its stomach. Sucking entails a very real exertion, and the muscles of the child's jaws are fatigued by the time it has satisfied its hunger. With regard to the amount of artificial feeds, the best plan appears to be to put 4 oz. of the prepared food into the bottle and let the child take what it wants; provided that the teat imposes on the child a sufficient exertion, it will never take more than it needs.

As the child grows older the quantity put into the bottle must be increased, and its quality gradually improved. At birth, the proportion suitable for most infants is one of cow's milk to two of water or barley water. The diluent should be gradually decreased until at six months of age the child is taking pure milk.

CHAPTER III

ARTIFICIAL FOODS AND ANTI-SCORBUTICS

AMONG the earliest of artificial substitutes for fresh milk must be reckoned the various brands of *condensed or preserved* milk, and of these preparations new varieties are constantly appearing. Condensed milk consists essentially of good fresh milk carefully prepared, and deprived of its water to a greater or lesser extent. Some, such as Nestlé's milk, retain the fluidity and other obvious characteristics of milk, but there are also preparations of *desiccated* milk from which practically all the water has been driven off. Condensed milk may be sweetened or unsweetened, and both are good. Probably the sweetened variety is more suitable for infants, and certainly if the unsweetened be used, cane sugar or milk sugar must be added. In many instances infants appear to thrive well on condensed milk, but it should not, if possible, be used exclusively, nor for too long a period. It contains all the constituents of a proper diet, and yet it has undergone some subtle change that makes it not only far less valuable than human milk, but also less valuable than fresh cow's milk when that food can be procured in a really good condition.

Some babies, however, appear to be unable to digest ordinary milk or condensed milk, and for them recourse must be had, at any rate for a time, to one of the modern substitute preparations, such as Albulactin, or Glaxo, or even the time-honoured albumin water. The two former are patent preparations, carefully and reliably made, which fill a useful although a subordinate place in the dietary of infants deprived for a time of more natural food. Albumin water, which is especially useful in some cases of illness, consists of white of egg well whipped up and mixed with previously boiled and cooled water in the proportion of 1 to 8 down to 1 to 6 parts.

Into this mixture, as Sir Thomas Barlow says, " one may soon begin to sneak a little cream," a useful addition, since no fat (one of the essential elements of human diet) exists in white of egg.

Natural milk, untreated in any way, as it exists in the human breast, or as it is drawn fresh from the cow, has in itself some property that is anti-scorbutic, but sterilised and pasteurised milk, and all the artificial foods, fail more or less in this characteristic. In order to remedy the deficiency it has been found useful to add to each feed, or to two or three feeds in the day, a few drops of *fresh-meat juice* (Appendix, Formula 11), or to give from twenty to sixty drops of *orange juice* in water two or three times a day. Both these devices assist in nutrition, and the meat juice is specially useful in the case of anæmic and fragile babies.

The feeding of infants over six months of age will be considered in Part V., Chapter I. (p. 218).

CHAPTER IV

THE NURSERY—TEETHING—VACCINATION— CIRCUMCISION

The nursery.— An important point in the rearing of any child is the preparation of its nursery. In the homes of the well-to-do no difficulty should arise; a fair-sized, cheerful room having one or more windows looking south or west should be selected. Its walls should be painted a pale-pink or pale-green colour, and the ceiling should be papered. Care should be taken that the boarding of the floor fits accurately, or failing this that it is adequately caulked. The boards should be covered with a cork carpet, not too dark in colour and fitting accurately. Rugs should be provided, one of them at any rate large and square, on which the child can sit and play. The room ought to be lighted by electric light when this is possible. Electric light is both cleaner and less heating than is gas, it is also less dangerous, for it does not escape, and is therefore less liable to cause explosions. Care must, however, be exercised to inspect the wires, at any rate twice a year, because should they become frequently damped, or their covering be worn away, there is a danger of fire.

The furniture of the nursery should be extremely simple. A strong, firm table, large enough to seat four to six persons, will serve for meals and for the purposes of a work-table. Suitable chairs should be provided for the nurse and for the children. In addition to this, the nurse should have two or three chairs for her own use and each child should have its own chair, low in the seat so that the little legs can reach the ground, and comfortably adapted for the support of its back. The provision of a small table to match the chair gives the child great pleasure, but probably this can only be managed in a large nursery. Cupboards with two shelves and a flat top, not more than 80 inches in height, provided with well-fitting doors and suitable divisions, will be found useful. One portion can be devoted to nursery linen and stores, a second to nursery crockery and other utensils, and a third should have smaller subdivisions, one of which may be assigned to each child, who from an early age should be expected to put away its toys and books. The fireplace, which should be provided with a slow combustion stove and broad tiled-hearth, should be defended by a high fireguard, the meshes of which are sufficiently close to prevent children's clothes or hands from being burnt. The room will not be complete without a few pictures on the walls. These should be copies of masterpieces, and should represent scenes in which children can take an intelligent interest, and the picture over the mantelpiece should be of a distinctly religious character, whether the subject be drawn from the Old or the New Testament.

The night nursery should also be a large airy room very similar to the day nursery. The furniture should be simple and scanty. A sufficient provision of beds, a washstand and dressing table for the nurse, and cupboards sunk in the wall are preferable to wardrobes and chests of drawers, and there should be one or more miniature washstands for the use of the children. Where possible, a separate bathroom should be devoted to the use of the nursery folk, and the bath should not be enclosed by boarding, for that involves a dead space from which dust cannot be excluded. The bathroom should be furnished with hooks for clothing, and with a press, or, better still, an airing cupboard, to contain the nursery bed-linen, etc.; and in one corner should stand a proper baby's bath, the porcelain of the bath being sunk in a wooden framework of convenient height. This bath is useful, at any rate up to the end of infancy, as the child may need to be washed by the nursery fire when it is ailing or the weather is cold.

All windows in nursery domains should be

fitted with Hinckes-Bird boards, which by raising the lower sash cause an over-riding of the upper and lower portions of the windows ; this secures permanent ventilation. If there be too much draught, or should smuts enter, a layer of gamgee tissue can be laid in the opening and renewed every few days.

Eruption of the teeth.—The young mother usually looks forward to the teething of her first child with considerable fear, and indeed the acute periods of teething are more or less troublous times for all concerned.

The difficulty, however, does not arise so much from the absolute cutting of the teeth as from the fact that great developmental changes are in progress, and that the child's condition is therefore one of unstable equilibrium. In infancy, the influence of the spinal cord is in excess of that of the brain, and there is therefore a greater liability to fits of convulsions following on relatively slight stimulation. Luckily, a fit of convulsions in infancy does not necessarily mean anything like so grave a constitutional disturbance as it does in later childhood or in adult life ; indeed, the convulsive fit which frequently announces the commencement of one of the acute infectious fevers is strictly analogous to the shivering which announces the same infection in an adult.

It is to be remembered that the first set of

teeth, the *milk teeth*, are already developed in the jaw when the baby is born, and that therefore the old idea that the baby was bound to be restless and unhappy during the period which was called the " breeding of the teeth " has no foundation in fact. When the infant is born the gums are firm and indeed somewhat hard, but the form of the teeth is seldom visible until later.

The teeth grow and press on the tissues of the gum, which are gradually absorbed before them. The process is not pleasant to the child, the gum becomes swollen, hot, and very tender, sucking ceases to be a pleasure, and sleep appears to be both less sound and less refreshing. A slight degree of feverishness frequently exists, and the lessened appetite is a blessing in disguise. The child should be allowed to drink freely of water, which may be sweetened with a little glycerin in cases where the child is constipated. Constipation is, indeed, a frequent accompaniment of the acute stage of teething, and always demands careful attention, for the presence in the blood of toxins derived from the bowels in addition to the mechanical irritation caused by hard and dry fæces, adds greatly to the child's discomforts and poorliness. A little more orange juice, or the addition of some preparation of malt to the diet, may suffice, but if not an occasional grain of grey powder at night, followed by a dessertspoonful of fluid magnesia in the morning, will probably afford relief. If the sluggishness appears to exist chiefly in the lower bowel, and the presence of a hard dry mass is suspected, the introduction of a cacao-butter suppository, or the injection of a tablespoonful of olive or castor oil, will afford great and immediate relief.

In consequence of indigestion and constipation, some babies suffer during teething from a red and irritating rash which adds greatly to their discomfort. It should be treated by strict attention to the stomach and bowels, and by powdering the surface with one of the many innocent dusting powders sold for babies' use.

Frequently, in connection with this rash there is well marked irritation in the folds of the knees, elbows, armpits, and more especially in the groins and about the external generative organs. The skin in these positions is so tender and easily frayed that it readily becomes sore and even moist. Much relief may be afforded by use of the ointments set forth in the Appendix (Formula 7), or, in cases where greasy preparations do not suit, by the use of calamine dusting powder or Emol Keleet. An attempt to relieve the annoyance of the rash may also be made by the administration of a teaspoonful of fluid magnesia, three or even four times a day. So long as the rash continues the parts affected should not be washed too frequently, but should be kept scrupulously clean by means of vaseline, cold cream, or hazeline snow, and the clothes should be changed as often as may be necessary. Olive oil soap or Castile soap is good for nursery use.

Sometimes a teething baby suffers much from diarrhœa, but in the majority of instances the looseness of the bowels is not directly attributable to the teething, except in so far as teething may be the cause of the precedent constipation. It is more likely that it is due to errors in feeding, to want of adequate attention to the food and the feeding bottle, and all these matters must be set in order at once. The best treatment for the ordinary diarrhœa of infants consists in the administration of an eggspoonful of castor oil. The child readily takes this drug when well mixed with a teaspoonful of hot water sweetened with a little castor sugar or glycerin.

The nervous troubles incidental to the teething period are certainly the most dreaded and are doubtless the most serious. Quite short of convulsions there may be a good deal of twitching of the muscles and contortion of the features. Sometimes there is a fairly rigid folding of the thumbs into the palms of the hands, a transient squint, or a peculiar up-rolling of the eyeball. The child is unnaturally fretful and peevish by day, nothing seems to satisfy it, and much patience and good humour are demanded from mother and nurse. The child does not sleep so well as usual, and indeed sometimes sleeps but little for several nights together. In these cases a careful review must be made of the whole of the child's circumstances, and anything that is found wrong must be at once corrected. If the nervous disturbance persists or increases a doctor should see the child, but where no doctor is available and the ordinary magnesia or oil fails to give relief a small dose of bromide of potassium may be given at bedtime for several nights, or even twice to three times in twenty-four hours when the nervousness is very great. The dose for a child from six to twelve months old is from 2½ to 5 grains. A 5-grain tabloid should be dissolved in a wineglassful of water and more or less of it be given for one dose. The amount of water appears to be large, but the bromide would cause considerable local irritation in the stomach if not suitably diluted. Infants bear the administration of the bromides very well, but they bear all preparations of opium very badly, therefore *no* soothing syrups or teething powders should be given, except under a doctor's advice.

The **convulsions** of infancy greatly resemble an ordinary epileptic attack, but they differ from it inasmuch as there is no premonitory cry. The child, who may have seemed poorly and ill at ease for a few days, or who, on the other hand, may have appeared to be in perfect health, suddenly turns pale, becomes rigid, the face and limbs begin to twitch, the eyeballs roll upward, probably a squint appears, and then commence wild and disorderly movements of the limbs and body. The attack appears to be extremely alarming, but does not last long. When a mother says that her child has been convulsed for half an hour, an hour, or any longer space of time, it is to be understood that the child has suffered from a succession of fits. If there be one isolated attack only, the child soon recovers consciousness; but when there are many in rapid succession it remains more or less comatose for a variable time.

Similar convulsions frequently occur in children under the same circumstances in which adults suffer from delirium or rigors; i.e. they occur under the influence of the poisons generated in various acute infections, and sometimes after accident and injuries. Also, symptomatic convulsions may occur in the course of such chronic illnesses as kidney and brain disease.

The usual treatment for a fit of convulsions is to put the baby into a really warm bath and pour a gentle stream of cold water over its head and face from a sponge; but although this may very properly be done, the best treatment is to give the child first an emetic and then a purge in order to remove all offending material from the stomach and bowels. Subsequently, if the child twitches or is restless, one full dose of bromide of potassium may be given. An early opportunity should be taken of examining the mouth and gums. If the eruption of a tooth or teeth appears to be imminent and some part of the gum is red and swollen, it must be lanced. This is a doctor's business, and, indeed, it is probable that where the services of a doctor are readily obtainable one will already be in attendance on the sick child; but where no doctor is at hand the lancing of the gum can be readily performed by the father or mother. The infant's mouth should be well cleaned with boric-acid lotion (Appendix, Formula 12), then the gum should be firmly held between the finger and thumb, and a cut made with the point of a sharp knife or lancet until it is felt to grate against the hard edge of the tooth. If the tooth be one of the front teeth this will suffice; but if it be one of the back teeth a similar cut should be made across the gum at a right angle to the first. There is no fear of injuring the child in any way, and the relief obtained is usually great.

Night terrors. — Closely allied to convulsions is a remarkable condition that may occur towards the end of the first dentition, but which

Teething

is more frequent in children who are rather older. The child wakes up in a great state of alarm, screaming and excited; the condition is very peculiar: the child appears to be entirely occupied with a terror the cause of which is not apparent to anyone but itself. While the attack lasts the little victim does not seem to hear—and certainly does not understand—anything that is said; the eyes are wide open and staring, but the child does not see, or at any rate does not recognise, anyone near it. In this case the immediate treatment must be the application of some sharp stimulus from without, such as sprinkling the face with cold water, or a smart slap on the bare buttock. When once the child's attention has been recalled to the really existing circumstances the attack is at an end, and it will soon be asleep again. Just as in the case of convulsions, the deep cause of night terrors is the temporary instability of the nervous system due to rapid development, and the immediate cause some irritant, such as unwonted excitement of the brain by pleasure or pain, or the familiar irritation of stomach or bowels.

Tetany. — Yet another nervous ailment, common in little children, especially during the teething period, is known as tetany. It is a simple trouble and not to be mistaken for the very grave disease known as tetanus. It is a peculiar kind of spasm chiefly affecting the neck, hands, and feet, and more especially the fingers and thumbs. As is the case with most other convulsive and nervous affections, tetany is commonest in nervous and rickety children. Its treatment presents no special features, but consists in great care of the general health and the avoidance of all irritants, both of mind and body. Tetany is not dangerous, but the spasms are evidently painful to the child, and are alarming to the mother.

Asthma of Millar.—This is a peculiar nervous ailment common enough during the first dentition, and generally known as *child-crowing*. It occurs most frequently during a fit of crying; the child holds its breath, turns black in the face, and is manifestly much alarmed. So, too, is its mother, and, indeed, the infant looks as if it were dying. However, after a few seconds, that appear to the anxious watcher as if they were hours, there is a long, whistling, indrawn breath, the horrible spasm of the throat relaxes, and the child's colour becomes natural as air gains access to its lungs. Death very seldom occurs, such a fatality being among the curiosities of medicine. Like all other nervous troubles, prevention is the best cure for child-crowing. When it occurs it should be treated much in the same way as night terrors, by affusion with cold water and a hearty smack behind.

Teething

Affections of the gums. — One of the commonest troubles during teething is, very naturally, undue swelling and redness of that part of the gums where the eruption of a tooth or teeth is imminent. The painful part may be gently rubbed with glycerin and borax, or honey and borax. Sometimes the child appears to derive comfort from biting anything; in such cases a rubber ring should be provided, but care must be taken that it does not fall on the ground or get otherwise soiled, and it should be boiled at any rate once a day. In no case should a *comforter* be used; it is a mere indulgence, whereas the occasional use of a hard ring is medical treatment. In cases where the distress and inflammation are very great, the remedy is the lancing of the gum as described above (p. 198).

Sometimes the teething infant suffers from small superficial ulcers on the inside of the cheeks and gums. These are usually digestive in origin, and should be treated by careful attention to diet and to the condition of the stomach and bowels.

Another trouble, chiefly seen in sickly or neglected children, is *aphthæ*, so-called *thrush*. The mucous membrane of the mouth and gums is studded with small milk-white patches. These can be removed with a camel's-hair brush or with a finger wrapped in a clean piece of linen. It will then be seen that the mucous membrane below is red, raw, and superficially ulcerated. In bad cases there is much inflammation round the patches, and the child's health suffers severely. Sometimes a similar condition is observed around the anus, and also on the vulva of female infants; this is what is known as the "thrush going through," but there is no reason to suppose that the whole length of the alimentary canal is affected; it is more likely that the spores of the minute fungus which causes the disease have been conveyed by the fingers of the child's attendant. It is to be remembered that this condition is extremely infectious, and that when one child of a family is suffering from it the greatest care should be exercised to isolate not only the child but all clothes, towels, and utensils that are used for it. The teething baby generally dribbles much, and the saliva which thus flows over towels, clothes, toys, etc., is the real infecting agent. It ought to be unnecessary to say that babies should never be kissed on the mouth or face, for thrush and still more serious ailments are thus readily conveyed. In healthy infants thrush is not a very serious disease, but in neglected cases and in sickly children not only must it be looked upon as an important symptom of their condition, but it must also be remembered that the soreness and inflammation of the mouth prevent the child from taking its food in comfort, and are likely to lead to a refusal to suck.

The treatment of thrush should be both general and local. It will frequently be found that a change of diet is desirable. A reference to the weight chart, which should always be most carefully kept, will probably show that the infant is not gaining in weight as it ought to do, and very likely a certain amount of softness of the flesh and pallor of the complexion may be noted. Some change should therefore be made in the diet, anti-scorbutics should be administered, and perhaps a tonic will be ordered. In such cases small doses, 5 to 10 drops, of Parrish's food, or half a teaspoonful of malt with iron will be useful. Locally, the mouth should be kept very clean ; it should be washed with a chlorate of potash lotion (as much powdered chlorate of potash as will dissolve in cold water may be safely used), and after the washing the sore spots should be painted with glycerin and borax.

Urinary troubles. — It will be noticed that in some teething infants there is an excessive secretion of urine. The kidneys work too hard, and very frequently the bladder is irritable. In consequence the unfortunate child is never dry, and there is a great risk of most uncomfortable chafing and soreness of the buttocks, the inner side of the thighs, and all adjacent parts. The only remedy is to keep the child as dry as possible and to apply boric-acid vaseline, cold cream, hazeline snow, or some other soothing ointment.

In some cases where the urine is less abundant it will be noticed that the napkins are stained pinkish-yellow, and—more especially in boy babies—there may be in the urine occasional red dots resembling cayenne pepper. These are crystals of *uric acid*, sometimes known as *gravel*. The child's diet should be regulated, broth and soup being omitted; much barley water and plain cold water should be administered, and the bowels kept fairly relaxed.

Vaccination.—It is difficult to understand how any intelligent person can object to vaccination. It is fashionable among a certain group of people nowadays to suggest that it is a cruelty and a relic of barbarism. If, however, they would read family histories as recorded on the fly-leaves of old Bibles, they would find many records similar to that of a family named Skinner, where of fourteen children born to the couple, eight had smallpox and six of the eight died of it. Early in the nineteenth century, so heavy was the incidence of smallpox, so great its fatality, and so disabling and disfiguring were its results in those patients who survived, that in many instances a man refused to marry a girl who had not already had the disease, the reason being that if she had had it the extent of the evil was known, but if she had not a few years might find the young man a widower, possibly with helpless children, or saddled with a wife who was blind, deaf, or at any rate sadly disfigured.

People who conscientiously object to vaccination should consider that if two or three vaccination pustules appear to them to be so formidable, how much more serious must the condition be when there are two or three hundred pustules, many of them situated on the face and eyes. We should all carefully remember that smallpox is violently infectious, readily conveyed from person to person, and even conveyed by the air, by flies and dust, from the sick to the healthy. When once smallpox develops we do not know of any method to cut short the illness, but efficient vaccination and re-vaccination afford an almost certain preventive; therefore, in the interests both of the infant and of the community, every child should be vaccinated within the first few months of birth. According to law the child must be vaccinated within six months unless a duly qualified doctor certifies that it is in such a condition of health as to make vaccination undesirable for the time being. Such a certificate can only postpone vaccination for two months, but of course it may be renewed if necessary. A parent who *conscientiously objects* to vaccination on the ground that he believes it to be dangerous to his child may obtain an exemption order from the magistrate; but in view of the relative effects of vaccination and smallpox it is difficult to understand how *conscientious* objections can exist.

Every mistaken opinion must have some foundation, good or bad. In the case of objections to vaccination it is likely that they are founded, first, on the belief that some serious disease, such as syphilis or tuberculosis, may be conveyed in the vaccine lymph. Secondly, it is undoubtedly true that in some instances vaccination causes much local sepsis, and even a certain amount of constitutional disturbance. The reply to the first objection is that at the present time calf lymph is invariably used, and that the calf is not liable to be affected by syphilis; also that lymph is so carefully collected from the calf that no blood is drawn, and that the pure lymph is unable to convey any disease except *vaccinia*, the condition which it is designed to convey. With regard to the second objection, " bad arms " would cease to exist if the part were carefully cleansed beforehand, and if immediately after the vaccination a vaccination shield, or other suitable means, were used to prevent the part from being rubbed, and also to prevent the accidental contamination conveyed by the child's clothes, by dust, and by insects. Equal vigilance is demanded of the vaccinator. The

Vaccination

vaccine tube should not be broken until the last moment, and the needle or lancet used for the tiny operation should be sterilised by passing it two or three times through the flame of a spirit lamp.

No doubt the opposition to vaccination originated in the employment of arm-to-arm vaccination, with failure on the part of operator or parents to secure adequate cleanliness. These errors are easy of remedy, but the failure of parents to have their children vaccinated constitutes a national danger. It is amusing, as well as pathetic, to note that when there was a small epidemic of smallpox in 1902 thousands of conscientious objectors went privately to strange doctors in towns far away from their own to secure the protection which they had condemned.

Vaccination ought to be done in the upper part of the left arm. Some foolish people prefer to have it done on the leg. The leg of the incontinent infant is much more liable to contamination with septic matter than is the upper arm, and in the case of a child who is able to walk there is a difficulty in securing quiet rest during the seventh, eighth and ninth days after vaccination, when the pustules have formed and are surrounded by a ring of inflammation.

The management of a child after vaccination is extremely simple. Probably nothing will be noticed until the fifth or sixth day after the little operation, then a tiny vesicle resembling a pearl may be seen at each point of insertion. These vesicles grow rapidly and are soon surrounded by a pink halo. By the eighth or ninth day the contents of the vesicles are turbid and yellowish, the swelling and redness increase, the child may be a little feverish, restless, constipated, and unwilling to take food. All this trouble is at its height about the ninth, tenth and eleventh days; then the vesicles burst, and a little honey-like fluid exudes; the inflammation quickly subsides, the pocks become brownish, and finally greyish-black, they quickly cease to trouble the child and shrink in area, and a thick black crust drops off about the end of the third week, leaving a depressed white scar from one-third to one-half an inch or rather more in diameter.

All through this time it is necessary to protect the arm from injury and from dirt. The child's diet will probably need to be a little thinner than usual, and plenty of water or barley water should be given. The condition of the bowels must be carefully watched, and probably a dose of castor oil followed by two or three of fluid magnesia may be given if the child is feverish or restless. It is quite true that a certain amount of inconvenience is suffered, both by parent and child after vaccination, but it

Circumcision

is as nothing compared with the dangers and miseries of smallpox.

It is to be remembered that the benefits of vaccination last in full force for about seven years and then gradually decline, hence the need for re-vaccination before puberty and again towards the end of adolescence.

Phimosis. — In the case of male infants, the mother or nurse may sometimes notice that the child is restless and cries before he passes water. If then she looks at the little penis, she will see that it swells and very likely becomes curved just as a flexed finger is curved. On further examination she will see that the organ is covered with a skin which becomes greatly stretched at the time of micturition, and also that its opening at the end of the organ is so small that the extremity of the penis cannot protrude nor can the skin be pushed back off it. This constitutes the condition known as phimosis. Not infrequently the child's life is rendered miserable by the frequently recurring difficulty and pain, and sometimes it is sufficient to cause injury to the bladder. In addition to these considerations, when the boy grows older the constant irritation is likely to lead to frequent handling of the part and to futile attempts at pulling the skin loose. Phimosis, therefore, all too generally leads to habits of self-abuse in the growing boy, and thus a grave moral injury is inflicted. Later on in life the man's relations with his wife may be rendered imperfect and even extremely painful by a tight condition of the foreskin (prepuce), and all through life the very necessary cleanliness and toilet of the part is impossible. In consequence of this, the natural secretion does not find sufficient vent, it dries and hardens between the prepuce and the exquisitely sensitive surface beneath, and the soreness and discomfort thus produced cause so much irritation and handling as to lead in the first place to masturbation and later on to fornication.

Paraphimosis.—In some cases a further complication arises where the orifice is not quite so small. The prepuce can then be pushed back, but some unlucky day the extremity of the organ, called the *glans*, swells, and the prepuce cannot be returned to its proper position. Very great discomfort and considerable swelling result, and the need for surgical help becomes urgent.

In all cases of phimosis, and still more where paraphimosis exists, the little operation of *circumcision* should be undertaken. Occasionally, when no doctor is at hand, temporary relief may be given by stretching open the orifice of the prepuce by means of a pair of fine forceps, or by giving a tiny snip to the front surface of the stretched membrane with a pair of scissors. It

Circumcision

is, however, very undesirable for anyone un-
acquainted with anatomy to interfere with so
delicate an organ. Tender-hearted mothers need
not be afraid for their babies to be circumcised ;
they should remember that under the Jewish
law, every male infant is circumcised on the
eighth day. In the olden days, the Jewish rite
was performed by men who had no anatomical
knowledge and who took no antiseptic precautions, yet evil consequences were rare, and nowadays, when the child receives all proper care
and attention, there is nothing in the operation
which should alarm the most timid. The fact
that the baby is ready to take the breast as
soon as it awakes from the anæsthetic, and
that its sleep is in no ways disturbed, shows
that it suffers little either locally or nervously.

In each case of circumcision, the doctor who
does the operation will give the necessary directions for after-care, but it must be carefully
remembered that in no case should the gauze
wrapped round the tender organ be pulled
off ; it will come away spontaneously and comfortably if the child is held for some time in a
bath of warm water. Should the gauze stick
more than usual, it may be rapidly separated
by the application of dioxygen or some similar
preparation of peroxide of hydrogen.

Should the child be restless and uncomfortable,
extra water or barley water may be given to

drink, and the bowels must be very carefully supervised. Infants are scarcely ever sore after circumcision, bigger boys may be, and in cases where the operation has unfortunately been postponed, all meat, poultry, and fish, together with animal broths and soups, should be avoided for a week or ten days.

The boy's comfort will be promoted by sitting in warm water night and morning, by the careful greasing of the part with a soothing ointment (Appendix, Formula 7), and also by the protection of the tender part by a mass of cotton wool held in place by a loose diaper. In older patients the weight of the bedclothes should be kept off by means of a cradle, such as is used to protect either body or limbs after operations.

PART V

THE MOTHER IN "THE NOISY YEARS"

CHAPTER I

THE CARE OF YOUNG CHILDREN

THE mother's duty towards her little children may be considered in three age-periods. Infancy, which corresponds with the time of the first dentition, terminates at the age of two. Elementary school life begins at the age of five, leaving an intermediate period during which home management and care should lay a satisfactory foundation for the more definite and formal education that follows.

The period of infancy. —In preceding chapters much has been said about the early requirements of the infant, its dentition, and the troubles incident to the first few months of life. It is now desirable to consider the characteristics of a healthy baby at birth and the changes that these characteristics undergo with the lapse of time.

The healthy infant at birth weighs on an

The Seven Ages of Woman

average from 6½ to 7 lb., and measures about 19 to 20 inches in length. Male children are, on an average, slightly heavier and longer than female. The greatest difference between male and female infants is to be found in the superior size and hardness of the boy's head. This partly accounts for the greater proportion of stillborn males. Although the above weights and measures are correct for the average child, healthy infants may be born at full term whose weight does not exceed 5 lb.; a weight of 9 or 10 lb. is not uncommon, and occasionally children turn the scale at 14 lb. An American case is on record of a child said to weigh 18 lb. at birth ! When it is remembered that 18 lb. is the weight of an exceptionally fine child at six months of age, it is to be hoped that the story is not true, or that at any rate it is unique.

The healthy newborn infant is of a pleasant pink colour, there is a good development of fat, and its movements are vigorous. The eyes are bright, the hair varies in length and in colour, and the body, although sometimes covered with a soft, fine down, has but little of this covering when it is really robust. At birth the skin is smeared more or less abundantly with a greasy material known as *vernix caseosa*. This is removed by rubbing the child all over with warm salad oil before its first bath ; if a little remains it will cause no harm, but the child's tender skin must not be irritated and frayed by futile attempts to remove any portion that does not readily come away.

Among the signs of maturity are not only the characteristics noted above, but the perfection and length of finger and toe nails, which at full term should come quite to the end of the digits, and may sometimes project a little beyond them. At birth the eyes, although open and bright, appear to have little power of vision ; they do not fix anything, and probably at first even a bright light is not seen. Vision, however, develops rapidly, and after a time resembles that of the adult in being *binocular*, as is proved by the increasing definiteness and success of the child's efforts to touch and to grasp the objects before it. Quite equally the function of hearing, although no doubt existent at birth, quickly becomes stronger and more useful. The infant at first does not recognise voices ; it appears to know its mother or nurse by her smell, but after a time increasing accuracy of hearing is shown by the child's more or less successful efforts to repeat the sounds that it hears, while its growing intelligence is demonstrated by its evident recognition that certain sounds correspond with various external objects, and that certain other sounds may influence the conduct of other people.

It is to be observed that the sound *ah* is usually the earliest to be accomplished by the child, and that its vocabulary in very early days is limited to this vowel sound with certain precedent letters, and that it has a tendency to duplicate sounds ; thus are formed ma-ma, pa-pa, na-na, and da-da. These sounds appear to be common to children of widely differing races, just as are the clouded blue eye and the indeterminate colour of hair. Later on in infancy the vocabulary increases, other vowels and a greater variety of consonants are used. The child's intellectual development proceeds as rapidly as his power of phonation, and by the end of infancy short sentences of definite meaning can usually be formed. Some children are extremely backward in talking, and should they not acquire clear and ready speech by the age of three, it is probable that they may be found to be backward or deficient in other ways ; the question will then arise whether special methods may not be required to help their development. The human infant at birth is remarkably helpless ; its limbs move vigorously, but the power of direction appears to be wanting, for locomotion does not develop for several months. The child grasps strongly with its hands, and holds out its arms to mother or nurse long before any similar purposeful movement is made with the legs. In most children the power to crawl on all fours, or to get about with a peculiar shuffling movement, the child sitting on the floor and propelling

Care of Young Children

itself chiefly by its arms, may be seen somewhere about the sixth or seventh month. Next comes the power to pull itself into a more or less erect position with the help of table, chair, bed, or friendly hand. Small, light, but healthy children may run alone as early as ten months, while bigger and heavier children, especially those with well-developed heads, appear to be afraid to trust themselves until three or four months later. When it is remembered that the head at birth is pretty nearly a quarter of the total length of the child, and that a marked disproportion of top-heaviness persists, although in a lessening degree, all through childhood, it is not wonderful that the human infant is slow in walking and running.

The capacity for being pleased and amused appears pretty early in life, and a genuine smile of pleasure may be seen somewhere in the course of the third month. From this time onwards the dawning intelligence increases rapidly, and the little infant quickly learns to distinguish its mother's moods. Her approbation or disapproval is appreciated, and if she be consistent the child quickly becomes obedient. This dawning love of approbation and sense of duty may be turned to good account in accustoming the child to acquire cleanly habits. The little creature soon associates the physical sensations of bladder and bowel with the contact of its

little utensil and certain encouraging sounds
made by the mother. The sounds are diligently
imitated, and the function is performed, to the
satisfaction of both mother and child. Any
failure to maintain the standard is reproved
by the mother by gesture and by sound ; the
frowning face, the shaken finger, and the tone
of disapproval impress the docile pupil, are
frequently imitated, and nearly always acted
upon.

This period of infancy includes the highly
important time of the first dentition, for the lower
centre incisors (" front teeth ") generally erupt
somewhere about the seventh month, and are
quickly followed by their fellows in the upper
jaw. Next, after a little interval, come the
lateral incisors, most frequently the lower before
the upper. The first double teeth appear somewhere near the first birthday, and then there is
a considerable interval of rest before the eye
teeth appear, between the fifteenth and eighteenth
months, and finally, somewhere about the second
birthday the first set of twenty milk teeth is
complete.

The food, clothing, exercise, and sleep during
the interesting period of infancy proceed by a
gradual progression.

It will be remembered that the infant was
able to take pure milk at the age of six months,
and that from this time onwards a certain pro-

portion of farinaceous food may be safely added. There are many excellent artificial foods prepared for the use of infants. They may be divided into two great classes—(1) those intended for robust infants who are able to digest a normal amount of carbohydrates, such as those prepared by Savory and Moore, Allen and Hanbury, Neave's Food, Ridge's Food, Mellin's Food, and many others of equal value; and (2) those intended for infants whose digestive powers are below the normal, and whose food therefore must be more or less predigested. To this class belong Benger's Food, and all the varieties of peptonised milks and foods.

From the time that the grinding teeth appear some slight addition may be made to the infant's midday meal. The yolk of a poached or lightly boiled egg may be allowed two or three times a week, and broth or gravy, thickened with potato, rice, sago, bread, or toast, on the other days. Baked apple, the pulp of grapes freed from pips and skin, and orange juice will supply the necessary vegetable salts; while thoroughly well cooked and very milky puddings will round off a very perfect dietary. In the case of children of a constipated habit a teaspoonful of glycerin or honey once or twice a day will be found to be a better sweetening agent than sugar. Many authorities permit minced or scraped meat, chicken, or fish, from the age of one year; but there is no evidence to prove that this addition to the diet is of any advantage to the child.

The clothes of infants should be shortened as soon as they begin to acquire the power of independent locomotion; indeed, as soon as they begin to crawl, it is well for them to wear a garment similar to bathing drawers, which keeps their skirts safely out of the way and saves the child many tumbles. The general principles of good clothing, namely that it should afford adequate covering, sufficient warmth, and absolute convenience, should be borne in mind; care must also be taken that no tight garments or overdrawn strings cause the child inconvenience. The headgear of the child from six months to two years old must be regulated by the facts that it should protect the child's eyes from the glare of the sun and should also be soft enough to permit of the little one sleeping in the open air. A soft hat of quilted cotton or silk material will answer these requirements.

The hours of sleep gradually diminish as the child's interest in life and power of activity increase, but about twelve hours' sleep at night, and two or three in the day, are still necessary. The little one should be accustomed to go to bed with perfect regularity at a certain time. If the evening bath, followed by the evening meal, commences at six o'clock, it may be reckoned

Care of Young Children

that the child will be in bed and asleep by seven or earlier; if it can sleep until seven in the morning, a good night's rest will have been secured. It is desirable that the infant should be taken up when the mother goes to bed in order that the bladder may be relieved, otherwise the urine will pass while it is asleep, and it will be wet and uncomfortable, and consequently wakeful. In most instances the child will settle off again to sleep in a few minutes; if it does not do so a little drink of warm milk may be given, and the mouth should then be washed round with a fold of clean linen wet with boric lotion. Some children wake very early, and directly they awake this little entertainment should be repeated. A certain proportion of children will then sleep again, but those who do not must be taught to lie quietly in their cots and should not be taken into the mother's or nurse's bed.

Infants usually provide themselves with quite sufficient exercise, for during their waking hours they are in incessant movement and all the muscles receive the necessary opportunity of development. The infant, however, cannot secure fresh air for itself, but during the summer it should practically live out of doors, sleeping in a bassinette perambulator when inclined to sleep, and rolling about on a waterproof sheet during the waking hours.

The Seven Ages of Woman

Children from two to five years of age.
—Infancy ceases with the completion of the first dentition, and the official age for the close of this process is two years. School age begins officially on the fifth birthday, and this division of time corresponds well with the appearance of the characteristics and requirements of early childhood. The little child is now altogether more developed, more enterprising, and more intelligent than is the infant. This period of early childhood is one of great importance, and unfortunately it is probably one of the periods of a child's life which have hitherto suffered from a certain amount of neglect. Every mother and every nurse appreciate, at any rate to some extent, the unremitting care that must be bestowed on the infant, but some mothers and some nurses, to say the least, appear to think that when a child can walk and talk it does not need quite so much attention. As a matter of fact, there is no age throughout the long duration of human life that needs more care. The little child's muscular powers have all along been in excess of the wisdom with which it is able to direct them. The human child is unique in this respect; only after years of experience does it learn to avoid harmful and dangerous things — knowledge which comes instinctively to the young of other animals; consequently,

anyone in charge of beings so capable of incurring danger and so incapable of foreseeing and avoiding it must be constantly on the alert, and will find that for a satisfactory discharge of her duties she needs not only bodily vigour and quickness of perception, but also a loving sympathy and patience, failing which all her other gifts will be of little avail.

It is to be remembered that the little child is always making experiments, and that this leads it to put everything it possibly can into its mouth, with disastrous results if it be not carefully watched. The little child, also, cannot discriminate without experiment between a sharp steel knife and a blunt silver knife. Its experiments must be made, but it is not well for the child that they should be made without supervision. As a matter of fact, the healthy child between two and five years of age is really one person's work, and inasmuch as it is wasteful that the whole time of one adult should be thus monopolised, it is desirable, unless there are several children in the same nursery, that the child should be cared for in a day nursery or kindergarten.

The brain of the little child is extraordinarily active, and although, as said before, its reason and wisdom are not yet developed, its powers of perception and of memory evolve rapidly. No formal lessons should, therefore, be attempted until after the close of this period. On the other hand, the little ones should be trained in powers of observation; they should learn to distinguish between different colours and different coins, and to give a correct name to each. The older ones can be set to sort skeins of different-coloured wools, or to recognise the primary colours in different shades, as exemplified in fragments of silk or cotton materials. Little children greatly enjoy being shown pictures, but the pictures selected should be simple and broad in outline, artistic in drawing, and beautiful in colour. It is an open question whether comic and grotesque pictures are useful at this age, but most certainly no horrifying or vulgar illustrations should be shown to children. Much information may be given by this method; the names of parts of flowers and fruits, and many of the stories of sacred and profane literature, thus gain an entrance to the eagerly receptive minds and tenacious memories; short and easy hymns and poems become indelibly imprinted on the mind, but they are not *learnt* in the ordinary sense of the word, for the child makes no conscious effort to memorise.

Gradually during this age-period, and especially in its latter half, an invaluable beginning can be made in teaching the child as much as it can assimilate of its duty to God, its neighbour, and itself. Habits of obedience, punctuality and tidiness are acquired in many cases without effort; unselfishness and patience with others are more easily learnt at this age than they could be later on, and feelings of devotion, of reverence, and of love of God are readily evoked and will surely influence the whole life of the individual.

Mothers and nurses who are untruthful, capricious, and uncertain incur a very great responsibility, for as they are so will the children be, and as they train their little charges so will the next generation of men and women develop. It is of the very first importance that parents and guardians should not only have a reasonable household time-table, but should, so far as possible, observe it themselves and require a like punctuality in servants and children. From the earliest age, children should learn that food is eaten in order that the body may be strong and a fitting organ for the mind. The food provided should be plain but suitable and adequate, and no member of the family should eat cake, fruit, or sweets, except at the hours of meals. It is to be remembered that digestion is a continuous process, lasting on an average for three hours, and that the stomach requires an interval of rest between the final disposal of one meal and the ingestion of the next. It is also to be remembered that anything introduced into the stomach between meals interferes with the orderly process of digestion. The small supplementary meal is somewhat like an extra person who joins a group of sightseers being conducted round a cathedral or other place of interest ; either the new-comer is neglected or the original party must stand idle and fatigued while a hurried and imperfect attention is given to the intruder.

It is quite true that doctors sometimes order a glass of milk or cup of broth in the middle of the morning, but this is only done when there is a very considerable interval between breakfast and lunch, or when the child is unable to make a really satisfactory first meal. In no case can it be wise for sweets and similar interferences with digestion to be tolerated. There are not many sweets that are really fit for children, but those that are desirable should be given at the close of a meal, and not during the intervals.

Nocturnal incontinence of urine. — Up to the age of two years the tendency of the child to wet its bed is comparatively little noticed. Incontinence of urine is a characteristic of infancy, and although a careful mother will try to teach habits of cleanliness from the very first, she remembers that so long as the irritation of dentition lasts all children are liable to accidents. Unfortunately, in some cases the tendency to involuntary evacuation of the bladder persists not only into childhood but into adolescence, and sometimes even to adult years. Every effort should be made to check so annoying a habit as quickly as possible. A child must be roused once in three or four hours and given an opportunity to satisfy the wants of nature. In some young people, the accident does not happen once in three or four hours but once every night, approximately at the same time. In view of the danger of the habit becoming fixed, and greatly interfering with the comfort, the education, and the usefulness of the individual, it is quite worth while for some adult to sit up two or three nights in succession in order to note the exact time at which the accident occurs. When once this is known it is comparatively easy to rouse the child at the right time and so to prevent the formation of the bad habit. It will be sometimes noticed, that the child is dry so long as it lies on its side, but is incontinent as soon as it turns on its back. In such cases, the child should wear round its waist, next its skin, a handkerchief in which a tight knot has been tied in the middle. As long as it lies on its side it is comfortable, but when it turns on its back the pressure of the hard knot makes it quickly resume the better position. If the hard knot does not suffice, a large empty reel may be substituted. Older children and young people may be taught to listen to the warning of an alarum clock, but they must be cautioned that if once they fail to heed the alarum and lazily lie on in comfort, the warning after that will be in vain. Should these domestic remedies fail, it is well that a doctor should be consulted, so that, after careful local examination of the parts concerned, and also of the urine passed, suitable remedies may be ordered. In many instances, incontinence in boys is due to the need for circumcision (*see* p. 210). This is a strong argument in favour of the circumcision of infants, for a habit of incontinence of urine is a very serious handicap, both during school years and later.

Children from five to ten years of age. —During this age-period the little ones begin school education and make their first flight from the parent nest. It is a time of rapid growth and development both of mind and of body, and much care must be exercised that the children are not over-fatigued in any way. So far as the children of the leisured classes are concerned, it is usually better to avoid all formal lessons until the seventh birthday, although the informal training they have been receiving should be continued and may gradually become more difficult, more varied, and more interesting. With regard to the children of the poor, it is well that school age begins so early. The mothers are frequently very busy and are unable to give much time

and attention to their little ones. Long before
ordinary education is profitable, training both of
body and of mind should be carried out, and, as
already said, it is an economic waste for one,
two, or even three children to monopolise the
attention of an adult who could quite as easily
manage a larger number. Again, the solitary
child, whether rich or poor, misses the advantages
of companionship, with all that it connotes of
mutual discipline, of opportunities for delightful
games, and of stimulus to good behaviour.

Towards the end of this third age-period
definite intellectual work must begin. The
powers of memory are at their best, and such
pure efforts of memory as Greek and Latin
verbs and certain formulæ, such as the multi-
plication table, are acquired at this time with the
least possible exertion and strain. Naturally,
the instruction should be little by little, and
never pressed to the point of fatigue. Now,
too, is the time to form definite and systematic
training of the senses and muscles, and ball
games of all kinds gradually become both delightful and useful. The eye should be trained
to careful and accurate observation. To secure
this, a trayful of varied objects, from three to
twenty in number, should be shown to the
child for a minute or two and withdrawn;
the child should then be required to describe
each object as accurately as possible. Another

exercise is to reproduce with pencil and paper some object shown, or to copy simple diagrams whether of mathematical forms or outlines of leaves, fruits, and ordinary domestic articles. Great pleasure is given to children when coloured chalks or water colours take their appropriate share in this and similar exercises.

It must be carefully remembered that although the eye is an optical instrument which reaches perfection at the age of ten, yet the child's power of co-ordinating the finer movements of the hands and fingers has not yet been thoroughly trained. It should not, therefore, be required to read small type, to use small script, or to do fine sewing, knitting, crochet, etc. The use and the co-ordination of the finer movements can only come gradually, and the child from whom fine work is exacted will rapidly become both short-sighted and crookbacked. Great care should be taken at this time that children sit and stand in proper attitudes. There seems to be an innate but vicious tendency to sprawl when writing, very frequently with the head much too close to the paper, indeed almost resting on the left arm. In reading, either the child is apt to rest its head on both hands, which is clumsy and tends to the formation of a round back and flat chest, or the head is supported by one hand, which is even worse, because in this attitude the spine becomes crooked and the foundation of lateral curvature is laid. In standing, there is a great tendency to throw the weight of the body almost entirely on one leg, the other leg being extended laterally. This faulty position must be patiently and constantly corrected, for if persisted in it leads to deformity of the spine and pelvis, and is particularly injurious to girls.

Children during this age-period should never be allowed to remain seated at lessons for hours together. Even towards its close, an hour is much too long for any one class, and arrangements should be made for some simple exercises to be done with the arms and body while standing between the desks, and at least once in the morning a run in the garden, playground, or gymnasium should be allowed while the classrooms are thoroughly ventilated.

The clothing of children during these years may be very similar for boys and girls. Besides the ordinary underclothing, long stockings, knickers to the knees, and loose tunics or jerseys form a convenient indoor dress, to which overcoats may be added for outdoor wear when necessary.

Exercise at this time should be more systematised than in the earlier years. Dull and monotonous walks should be avoided, but walks for Nature Study are useful and delightful.

The Seven Ages of Woman

Besides this, a commencement may be made with ordinary gymnastic exercises, team games, and dancing, which are more fully considered in Part I., Chapter V. The ordinary walk, as conducted under the auspices of a nursemaid, cannot be too strongly condemned. Even if she be conscientious and well meaning she has not the necessary education or experience of life likely to make the walk really profitable and enjoyable to the children. If, on the other hand, the nursemaid is not a reliable young woman, the children are neglected while she gossips, reads a novel in the park, or gazes into the shop windows. In cases where other adequate exercise cannot be provided, the mother should herself take charge of the children's walk, or, where such an arrangement is impracticable, a thoroughly conscientious and well-educated girl should be engaged to take charge of several children and to play or walk with them for a certain number of hours daily. Such a girl is called in France and Italy a *trotteuse*.

Young children need long hours of sleep, not less than twelve at the commencement of this age-period, and the amount should be very slowly diminished, and quite up to the age of ten it should be the rule and not the exception for children to go to bed not later than seven o'clock.

CHAPTER II

THE CHILD IN SICKNESS

THE child in sickness is a pathetic little mortal.
The younger the child the more does its condition
approximate to that of a sick animal. At first
it has no words in which to describe its sufferings, and even later on in childhood the sufferings
are often misdescribed, and the pain is referred
to parts which are not primarily to blame. Thus,
in hip disease complaint is frequently made of
a pain in the knee ; in pneumonia, stomach-ache
is often an initial symptom ; while a decayed
tooth is sometimes responsible for headache, fever
and lassitude which might well be supposed to
betoken trouble in the brain.

From this inability to describe symptoms
arises the necessity for a very careful physical
examination of all sick children. The nurse
or mother should notice the colour of the child's
face, the equality or inequality of the pupils
of the eyes, the deviation of either eye from
the straight line, or any unusual movements of
the eyeballs. The examination of the mouth
and throat are of great importance ; the nurse
should sit facing the window with the back of

the child supported against her chest, and her arms should be ready to restrain its movements if necessary. The mother or doctor should stand in front of the child looking towards its face; the child, if old enough, should be asked to open its mouth, and if it has been well trained in habits of obedience there will be no difficulty about this, but if it be very young, very frightened, or very deficient in self-control, a finger should be passed into the mouth behind the teeth, or the necessary inspection must be secured by pressing with the thumb and finger on each cheek just in the line of the jaws. This pressure will force the child to open its mouth, and then a good view can be obtained of tongue, mouth, and throat by using a tongue depressor or the handle of a spoon. The examiner should be very careful to keep her own mouth shut while inspecting a patient's throat, otherwise infection of various sorts may be easily acquired. Should any of the child's saliva reach the examiner's eyes, face, or mouth, immediate disinfection must follow. As this examination of the throat is the most displeasing part of the process to the child, it should be left to the last.

A sick infant should be thoroughly undressed before examination, and so, too, should a child who is too ill to be annoyed by the removal of its clothes; but most children bitterly resent being undressed, and it is as well to do it by degrees. In any case, the examination should be made by the nursery fire, the child, if naked, being wrapped in a previously warmed blanket. When the child's chest is exposed the rate of respiration can be counted ; it is usually from twenty to twenty-four movements in the minute. The pulse-rate can be ascertained, either at the wrist or by the action of the heart, which can be felt by the hand laid flat on the left side of the chest. Infants soon after birth have a pulse-rate somewhere about 120 to the minute ; this should become progressively slower until during adolescence it gradually conforms to the adult's standard of seventy to eighty to the minute. The pulse-rate, however, is extremely variable, not only with age and with physical condition, but with every passing emotion and excitement. A temporary quickening of the pulse by ten or even twenty beats is of little importance, but more value is to be set on the quickening of the pulse which lasts for some hours and even persists during sleep.

In sharp contrast with the ready variability of the pulse is the persistence of the normal standard of temperature from birth throughout the whole of life. The normal line is drawn at 98·4° Fahr. ; anything lower than 98° is looked on with suspicion as showing a depression of vitality, while any persistent rise over 99° indicates feverishness. Even in disease variations of temperature usually occur within relatively small limits ; a fall of 2° to 2·5°, say from 98·4° to 96°, shows a dangerous condition of collapse, while temperatures above 105° are very uncommon, and any persistence above this is likely to prove fatal. Unusual temperatures, such as 108°, may occur as transient phenomena in certain diseases, but such an elevation is rare.

In adults the temperature is usually taken either in the armpit or in the mouth, but in infants and little children these positions are not very satisfactory. The child's axilla is so shallow that it is difficult to get a true registration of temperature, while the thermometer placed in the mouth is likely to be bitten in two. It is, therefore, better in very young subjects to pass the bulb of the thermometer well through the opening of the bowel. If very slightly greased it can be quite easily introduced with the child lying on its side. It is to be remembered that the ordinary temperature of the bowel is about one degree higher than that of the general surface of the body.

In addition to counting the respiration- and pulse-rate, the surface of the body should be examined to see whether any discoloration or rash is present. The shape and movement of the abdomen should also be observed, for a swollen, rigid, shiny and motionless abdomen probably means peritonitis, while in conditions

The Child in Sickness

of exhaustion and some forms of brain disease the abdomen looks hollow and is said to be *boat-shaped*. The buttocks, anus, and private parts of the child should always be carefully inspected, and any failure of ready movements of the arms and legs should be noticed.

The excreta of the child also call for observation. Discharges from the nose, mouth, throat and lungs should be received into absorbent paper handkerchiefs, which can be kept in a covered vessel for the doctor's inspection and then immediately burnt. It is surprising, however, how very seldom little children expectorate ; when they cough the discharge from the lungs or bronchial tubes rises into the throat, perhaps even into the mouth, but is immediately swallowed. It is sometimes possible to secure a little for purposes of examination by swabbing the back of the throat with absorbent cotton wool held in a pair of forceps. Vomit should always be looked at, and if necessary reserved for the doctor's inspection. Occasionally the contents of the stomach are coloured by fruit juice or other external colouring matter, which gives rise to the unfounded suspicion that the child is vomiting blood, and nothing but a doctor's examination will suffice to determine the truth.

Everything that passes from a child's bowel

237

must be carefully observed. The motions may be abnormal in quantity, in solidity, or in colour. People often think that diarrhœa exists because an unusual number of motions are passed in twenty-four hours. It is well to remember that the meaning of *diarrhœa* is a *running through,* and that therefore so long as the motions are solid it does not exist. The colour of the motions may be too light in cases of jaundice and whenever the liver is not acting sufficiently ; on the other hand it may be too dark from excess of bile, from the presence of blood, and when the child is taking certain medicines, e.g. iron, bismuth, and lead. In cases of colitis, inflammatory diarrhœa, dysentery, and worms the stools will often contain visible mucus in greater or less quantity. In colitis, casts of the bowel are not infrequent and are readily mistaken for portions of the bowel wall, and in the same disease, but more rarely, the patient sometimes passes masses of a peculiar gritty substance which has an abominable odour. In dysentery and inflammatory diarrhœa varying quantities of blood and mucus are generally present, and, in the worst cases, sloughy portions of the mucous membrane of the bowel, which cause the ejecta to have a most disagreeable and penetrating odour. Constipated motions are usually broken up into small, hard, dry masses, more or less of a chestnut shape ;

sometimes these masses are squeezed together by the pressure of the anus so as to form the normal cylindrical-shaped motion, but even then they quickly fall into their constituent parts. Not infrequently a constipated motion is smeared with old yellowish mucus owing to the irritation that it has caused in its passage along the bowel, and occasionally it may be noticed that the external portion of the lump is darker than the internal, having been discoloured by sulphuretted hydrogen gas during its delayed passage through the large bowel.

The urine of the infant is usually clear, colourless, and odourless, but as the diet becomes more varied the child's urine approximates more and more closely to the adult standard; it should be clear, sherry-coloured, and the odour not unpleasant. When the child does not take sufficient water, when it is feverish, and when during very hot weather it perspires much, the water tends to become scantier and at the same time deeper in colour. Sometimes under these circumstances there is more or less pinkish, reddish, or yellowish sediment. This last phenomenon is seldom seen in little children, but is not uncommon in adolescents who have a large appetite and sometimes rather overtax their digestive powers. On the other hand, the cayenne-pepper-like grains of uric acid are chiefly seen in the urine of male infants.

The Seven Ages of Woman

During the examination of a sick child the glands should be felt for about the neck, in the armpits, and the groins. Swollen glands that can be felt along the front edge of the *sterno-mastoid* (the big muscle which runs down each side of the neck from the base of the skull to the collar bone and breast bone) are those which most generally force themselves on the attention of parents. They may be, and very often are, tubercular, but their enlargement sometimes depends upon other diseases. Enlarged glands behind the angle of the jaw and under the chin are generally due to abnormal conditions in the mouth ; enlarged and septic tonsils and decayed teeth are responsible for most of these cases. Irritation of the scalp, whether due to lice, to rashes, or to sores, may cause enlarged glands, and under these circumstances some will be found quite at the back of the neck near the margin of the hair. Enlarged glands of different parts of the neck are frequently to be found during the course of diphtheria and German measles. When the glands of the axillæ and groins are enlarged the trouble may be due to some sore or wound in the corresponding limb, but if they be present in all four localities some general constitutional infection is probably present.

The sick-room, furniture, etc.—The description already given of a nursery (*see* p. 189) will

The Child in Sickness

serve very well for an ideal sick - room, only
the other children should be sent to other parts
of the house in all cases, and away from home
if the illness is infectious. It is practically
impossible to say during the first hours of any
illness whether it is a heavy cold or digestive
disturbance on the one hand, or measles, pneumonia, or other serious illness on the other;
therefore if a child appears to be ill and has a
high temperature and quick pulse it should
be isolated. This is a real difficulty not only
in the houses of the poor, but in the homes of
those whose means, although sufficient for a
comfortable ordinary life, do not readily provide
suitable accommodation in sickness. In all cases
of serious illness it would be wise for the children
of such families to be sent to hospital, where, in
many instances, those who can afford to pay a
small sum weekly can have more comfortable
accommodation than in the general ward.

There is much natural reluctance to send a
beloved invalid away from home. Many middle-
class parents have a certain proper pride and
dignity which revolt from partaking of anything in the nature of public charity. They resent
being indebted to the community and to the
doctors and nurses of public institutions for
the treatment which they would much rather
provide at home. However, in cases of serious
illness, home treatment is fair to no one; it

is impossible to command such excellent conditions as are provided both in the paying and in the general wards of the hospitals, and the little sufferer nursed at home is therefore handicapped in what may prove to be a life-and-death struggle. The parents themselves find that the care of a child who is very ill imposes on them anxious and laborious duties and broken nights that are incompatible with the father's daily work and the mother's duties towards other members of her family. The doctor is thankful enough to have serious cases in a hospital, where everything is easily provided, and where the House Surgeon's services are available night and day, so that valuable time is not lost should any sudden emergency occur. If, after all, it is decided to keep the child at home, special arrangements will have to be made to secure its safety and to guard against possible infection.

The ideal nursery, as previously described, will need very little alteration, only all surplus clothes, linen, toys, and books that may be in the nursery cupboards should be removed, and more than usual care should be taken to secure thorough ventilation and adequate means of regulating the admission of light. This may be done by the use of short curtains of casement cloth, preferably green in colour; they should slip on two or more rods so that the window may be shaded as required.

The Child in Sickness

The coals should be wrapped up in paper so that they may be placed noiselessly on the fire, and a stout walking-stick should replace the noisy poker. All utensils, whether for food or other purposes, should be washed in one of the nurseries or in the attached bathroom, and should on no account be mixed with those used by the rest of the household.

To avoid infection, sheets wrung out of a 1-in-20 carbolic lotion should hang over the doors of the sick-room, and anyone in attendance on the child should wear a long white overall or nightgown over her clothes. This overall should be left in the second nursery when she has occasion to leave the sick-room. Her hair should be covered with a handkerchief or cap, and she should be particularly careful to maintain her own health in as good a condition as possible. In cases of infectious disease she should wash her face and hands frequently, and if necessary gargle mouth and throat with Condy's fluid and water.

The floor should be cleaned daily by wiping it over with a broom, over which is tied a cloth wrung out of the carbolic lotion. The furniture should not be dusted, but wiped over with a damp cloth, and if the pictures are still in the room they should be similarly cleaned every day.

At the end of any infectious illness, the child,

its clothes, and its attendants must be disinfected, also the room and the furniture. The child's night clothes should be removed, and it should be rubbed all over with carbolised oil, wrapped in a blanket, and carried into the bathroom, where a thorough scrubbing from head to foot should be done. Clean warm clothes should then be put on, and the child should not return to the infected room. One such bath should not be considered sufficient; at least three should be administered, and in cases such as smallpox, chickenpox, and scarlet fever particular attention should be paid to the oiling and cleansing of the head, the hands, and the feet. Finally, if it be possible, the child should go away to the seaside or the country before mixing again with family and schoolfellows.

The child's attendant should disinfect herself in the same way, and be much in the open air before mixing with uninfected people.

The best purifier for rooms and furniture is prolonged exposure to fresh air and sunshine. In addition to this the floors, walls, and ceiling must be well rubbed with the wet carbolised duster, the woodwork must be washed and the windows cleaned, but the bedding if sufficiently valuable to be saved should be thoroughly *stoved*, that is to say, it should be sent away to some disinfecting station where it is subjected to great heat, sufficient to penetrate the whole thickness of bedding, blankets and eiderdowns.

As a matter of fact, even before the ordinary airing and cleaning of the sick-room, it should be chemically disinfected, either by burning in it a sufficiency of sulphur, or, more conveniently still, by the use of a formalin lamp. The bedding should be removed from the bedstead and set up so as to expose the entire surface to the action of the chemical; the doors and windows should be pasted up with strips of paper to retain the fumes in the infected room, and it should not be reopened for twenty-four hours, when it will be quite safe for cleaning.

CHAPTER III

THE COMMONER AILMENTS OF CHILDHOOD

INASMUCH as this little book is not a treatise on the diseases of children, it has been thought better not to give detailed descriptions of all the ailments common to young people. In the preceding chapter an attempt has been made to indicate the principles of nursing and the methods of examination of sick children, while in the present chapter a few of the commonest or most important of children's ailments are considered in detail.

Measles. —Measles is not only the commonest disease of childhood, but it is also the most fatal. More children die of measles than of scarlet fever and diphtheria together. This mortality depends in part on the fact that the disease is one of *little* children. They are attacked before they have a really good hold on life. Part of the great mortality is due also to accompanying bronchitis, a very serious disease in fat little children ; but the chief cause of the fatality is the fact that few people recognise the seriousness of measles, that fewer diagnose it early enough, and, chief of all, that so very few cases of measles are properly nursed.

Commoner Ailments of Childhood

Among the children of the well-to-do, measles is seldom fatal, and very seldom does it give rise to real anxiety. The one essential point of the treatment of measles consists in keeping the patient in bed in a warm room, with ample ventilation but no draught, and where the air is frequently made moist and soothing by the use of a bronchitis kettle. A bronchitis kettle is not a costly instrument, but a perfectly good substitute can be improvised by adapting a long tin tube terminating in a funnel to the spout of any big kettle. The use of the bronchitis kettle should be intermittent, for constant use would make the air too moist and enervating. A special mixture of Friar's balsam (Appendix, Formula 18) can be used in cases where the cough is frequent and irritable. In some cases inhalations of vapour of eucalyptus, a few drops only to a pint of tepid water, may be used, by means of an ordinary inhaler, or sprinkled on a cloth held a little distance from the child.

Symptoms of measles. — This disease begins very much as if it were an ordinary but severe cold, with much running from the eyes and nose, accompanied by a sensation of heaviness, illness, and stuffiness. The temperature, unlike that in an ordinary cold, rises steadily to 103° F. or thereabouts. On the third or fourth day the characteristic dull crimson rash appears in patches, first about the roots of the hair, and quickly spreads over the face, neck, and arms. On the second day of the rash it is to be seen all over the trunk, and the next day it appears on the legs. By this time the reddened, puffy face with its disfiguring eruption is becoming normal, and the whole rash quickly fades away. The superficial layer only of the skin loses its vitality, and after the completion of the eruption it is cast off in small bran-like flakes. This desquamation is extremely infectious, and therefore the whole surface of the body should be repeatedly oiled to prevent it from being widely scattered.

Bronchitis can scarcely be called a complication of measles; it appears to be of the essence of the disease, although in exceptional cases it is mild and may pass almost unnoticed. Sometimes pneumonia supervenes, but this is rare. Occasionally diarrhœa gives rise to trouble, and therefore the administration of fruit in measles should be scanty and cautious. Bleeding from the nose may occur, but seldom to a serious degree. In fact, the mortality of measles is chiefly due either to an accidental aggravation of the bronchitis, to some latent weakness in the child's constitution, or, most frequently of all, to want of careful nursing.

One often hears of *suppressed measles* and even of *hæmorrhagic measles*, but the suppression of the rash is generally due to the non-recognition of the disease and to consequent exposure to

Commoner Ailments of Childhood

damp and cold. In hæmorrhagic measles the rash is usually very abundant, dark purple or black in colour ; it appears to be due to a virulent form of infection, and is, of course, aggravated by want and exposure. An attempt must be made to save the child by immersion in a hot bath and the administration of some stimulant such as a teasponful or two of brandy, plenty of hot water, and sugar. Fortunately, this type of the disease is rare.

Rubella. — Rubella, otherwise called *Rötheln* or *German measles,* is a fairly common disease of childhood. It generally begins quite suddenly, a rosy, spotty rash appearing without previous illness. This ailment is distinguished from somewhat similar digestive and rheumatic rashes by the swelling and tenderness which occur in the glands of the neck. It may be accompanied by sore throat, headache, and other constitutional symptoms, but there is seldom cause for anxiety, and no permanent injury to health occurs.

The nursing treatment resolves itself into rest in bed and careful regulation of the digestive functions. Should any symptom be unduly emphasised, it must receive attention.

Influenza. — This extraordinarily multiform and tiresome disease may attack individuals of all ages. It may be of any degree of intensity, varying from a slight feverish catarrh to a most formidable and even fatal illness. Very unfortunately, influenza has no distinctive rash, although it may be accompanied by a rose-coloured eruption. There are two well-marked and several vaguer forms of this illness. In the commoner, and therefore better recognised, type of the disease it begins with the symptoms of an ordinary feverish cold ; there is much catarrh of the eyes, nose, and throat, and bronchitis often develops. The other prominent symptoms are headache, pains in the back and limbs, and digestive disturbances. The temperature rises, sometimes rapidly, and this, together with the other symptoms, may obscure the diagnosis between this type of influenza and measles, cerebro-spinal fever, and scarlatina. The diagnosis is soon cleared up, for the rash of scarlet fever should appear within the first forty-eight hours, and that of measles soon after the completion of seventy-two hours, while the symptoms of cerebro-spinal fever will quickly diverge from those of influenza.

In cases of a second well-marked type of influenza the stress of the disease falls chiefly on the stomach and bowels, and the sudden development of vomiting and diarrhœa may suggest acute dyspepsia or ptomaine poisoning.

In all cases of influenza the patient ought to go to bed immediately, partly in order to avoid the danger of infecting other members of the household, and partly to forestall the probable development of bronchitis. The ordinary domestic treatment for a feverish cold must be used, the bowels should be freely opened, the food should be light, nourishing, and digestible, the room well warmed and well ventilated, and the catarrh checked by inhalations as described in connection with bronchitis in measles (p. 247). If the fever be high, and still more if the pains in the limbs be distressing, moderate doses of aspirin (from 1 to 10 grains a day, according to age) may probably be ordered; or where weakness is a marked symptom from the beginning, quinine is useful. In the digestive form the diet will need to be limited to whatever the patient can most readily take, but should always be fluid and non-irritating.

Attacks of influenza of any type are often followed by an extraordinary degree of weakness. The apparently slight and short illness makes the patient feel as if it had lasted weeks. Under such circumstances tonics are needed, and a change of air is very beneficial.

Chickenpox. — The rash of chickenpox is generally noticed after the child has been ailing for twenty-four hours, but it is not infrequently a complete surprise. The small watery vesicles appear scattered on the body as if the child had been sprinkled with small drops of boiling water. There is sometimes a faint halo of redness about some of these spots. Constitutional disturbance is slight, and probably the child, if left to itself, would not go to bed. It is, however, better that it should do so. The bowels and diet should be regulated, and the child should be isolated for the sake of others.

Whooping - cough. — This complaint commences with a catarrhal period chiefly affecting the respiratory organs. At first it may be mistaken for a common cold, but instead of improving, the bronchial catarrh increases, and gradually the cough becomes more resonant and shows a tendency to be paroxysmal. After a time this nervous element is very well marked, and the cough becomes so violent that each paroxysm is accompanied by vomiting. The evacuation of the contents of the stomach is to be regretted, because it may interfere more or less with the child's nutrition, but the evacuation of mucus from the stomach and the respiratory passages is of great advantage. The fits of coughing vary greatly in number during the twenty-four hours ; it is well that a note should be kept of their number in order that progress may be observed. It is not necessary for children to be kept in bed for uncomplicated whooping-cough : when the weather is fine and warm they are better in the open air ; but great care must be taken to avoid damp and chill, and to prevent the infection from spreading to other children. Special care should also be taken to give the child a very

Commoner Ailments of Childhood

sufficient allowance of simple, nourishing food, but in the case of little children no meat should be given. It is also necessary to secure additional rest, especially should the child be delicate or nervous, and in those cases in which the disease is violent. Very little medicine is needed. Should bronchitis appear, it must be treated as in measles (*see* p. 247). The nervous element is best controlled by the administration of bromide of potassium, which, however, should be given under a doctor's directions. Many drugs have been recommended as specifics for whooping-cough, and perhaps quinine has some really beneficial influence. For older children two or three grains may be given in tabloid form, while for little ones small doses of the comparatively tasteless tannate of quinine or Martindale's really pleasant chocolate tablets of quinine may be substituted. The duration of whooping-cough is very variable, and when it unfortunately commences early in winter, the characteristic whoop may be heard until summer warmth returns.

Mumps.—This is an extremely painful feverish disease, the chief manifestation of which is great swelling and tenderness of the parotid gland, near the ear. This gives rise to an enormous and truly grotesque swelling of one or, possibly, both sides of the face. As a rule, the patient is quite unable to open the mouth or to talk with any comfort ; there is a real difficulty in getting enough to eat; and the patient feels most miserable and ill. Luckily the deformity, fever, and misery last only a few days, and usually subside without leaving any evil consequence behind them.

In exceptional cases the infection appears to spread to the generative glands, so that in boys the testes are swollen and painful, and in girls there may be pelvic pain and tenderness just above each groin, due to similar affection of the ovaries. These complications are a great annoyance, and add to the patient's sense of illness, but they are seldom dangerous. Hot fomentations or bran bags give some little relief, so, too, does a brisk purge. It is seldom necessary to keep the patient in bed, and the diet curtails itself, inasmuch as nothing but liquids can be taken. It is to be remembered that mumps is an extremely infectious disease, and the patient must be isolated for the sake of others.

Diphtheria. — Formerly diphtheria was greatly dreaded because it was one of the most fatal diseases. Indeed, up to quite recent years about one attack in three ended in death. Now, thanks to antitoxin, this mortality is greatly reduced; not more than 7 per cent. of those attacked die, and practically no one dies who has had an injection on the first day of the disease. The diagnosis of diphtheria is therefore a most important matter, but unluckily the commencement of the disease is generally insidious, and much precious time is often lost.

At first there is little to attract attention beyond pallor, and discomfort in the throat, the temperature does not run high, and the pulse is not very quick. At this time the throat may appear to be somewhat red, and resembles what is known as a relaxed throat, the patches of characteristic membrane not appearing until later. As a rule, the glands along the margin of the sterno-mastoid muscle, stretching from the base of the skull to the collar-bone, will be found to be enlarged, and frequently there is a certain amount of nausea or vomiting. After some few hours, or at most a day, the diphtheritic membrane appears. It is at first milky white and thin, but cannot be readily removed by a camel's-hair brush or pledget of wool because it is growing *in* the mucous membrane. The patches increase in size and in thickness, and become more firmly attached, the colour becomes yellower, and perhaps later on, owing to hæmorrhage, it may be dull, dark grey, or almost black. The membrane may be situated in any part of the throat, and the patches often run together over the surfaces of the tonsils and the uvula. As the disease develops the child's pallor and illness increase. The temperature does not necessarily run high, but may do so if an ordinary septic infection is added to the diphtheritic poison. In such cases the danger to life is greatly increased, as it is also in virulent cases, in which the membrane may extend in all directions—to the nose, the larynx, and the windpipe, causing much additional danger.

The two chief anxieties in an attack of diphtheria are the mechanical danger caused by the membrane growing into the larynx and causing death by suffocation, and secondly, the great depression of the vital powers owing to the poison generated by the minute organisms which cause the disease. An attempt is made to relieve approaching suffocation by the operation known as *tracheotomy*, and the equally deadly depression is met by stimulants and tonics. However, the really rational and efficient treatment of diphtheria is the early and, if necessary, repeated administration of antitoxin. In all cases in which diphtheria is suspected, a pledget of cotton wool must be rubbed on the mucous membrane of the throat, and should be sent forthwith for pathological examination. On this method of early diagnosis and the prompt treatment by antitoxin which it renders possible rests the child's chief hope of recovery. No other treatment can be substituted for it, and it is this alone which has so greatly reduced the mortality.

Those who nurse a case of diphtheria must remember that it is an exceedingly infectious disease, and that the patient and everything connected with the patient are capable of conveying the infection far and wide; very special care should therefore be taken to keep everything thoroughly disinfected.

Diphtheria sometimes leaves very serious consequences; the force of the poison expends itself chiefly on the heart, which is left feeble and incompetent for a long time. Fresh air, nourishing food, and heart tonics may be of real service; but it is also absolutely necessary that at first the patient should do literally nothing, and that all fatigue and over-exertion should be avoided until the heart has recovered its normal condition. In other cases the chief effects of the toxin are seen in troubles of the nervous system; squint may develop, and paralysis of one or more of the muscles of the eye; death may ensue from paralysis of the diaphragm, or paralysis of the limbs and other parts of the body may make the patient a helpless invalid for months. The earlier the antitoxin is administered the more likely is it that these disastrous sequelæ may be avoided.

Scarlet fever. — "Scarlet fever" is the English synonym for the Latin *scarlatina*, and not, as some people think, a graver form of the disease. This fever appears to have altered very much in type of late years, and is at present a much milder disease than it was fifty or sixty years ago. Quite possibly the benign type may pass away and scarlet fever may again become the much-dreaded scourge that it was in the middle years of the nineteenth century. Even now an occasional malignant case occurs, and children die from the violence of the poison before the rash has time to develop; also in a certain number of cases the poison, although not so immediately fatal, destroys life or cripples health by its toxic action on the heart, the throat, the glands, the ears, and other organs.

An ordinary uncomplicated case of scarlet fever commences more or less suddenly, headache, fever, vomiting, and sore throat being its prominent symptoms. Some time within twenty-four hours a very fine *dotted* or *stippled* rash appears; it may be looked for behind the ears, and on the forehead and cheeks, but it generally leaves a peculiar pale area round the mouth. The broad effect of this punctiform rash is that of a general bright pink or scarlet redness, which very quickly covers the whole body. If the throat be examined when the patient first complains that it is sore it will be seen to be swollen and covered with red dots. The tongue is said to be a *strawberry tongue*, but if so it is a white strawberry with red points. The glands in the neck are generally swollen, more especially those about the angles of the jaw, which are infected from the tonsils.

The temperature generally runs high; it is

Commoner Ailments of Childhood

irregular, but generally falls a little in the morning. Scarlet fever is one of the diseases in which unusually high temperatures may occur, but if not persistent they are not necessarily an indication of extreme danger. The patient complains chiefly of sore throat, headache, backache, sickness, and pains in the limbs. Delirium may occur, and used to be very common, but is less frequent at the present time.

The patient should be kept in bed on a milk or milk-and-broth diet, the hair should be cut short or shaved in all but the mildest cases, and the whole body thoroughly greased with carbolised oil or eucalyptus oil daily. Should the temperature be abnormally high, cool or cold packs and even baths may be necessary. It must, however, be remembered that after septic sloughing of the throat inflammation of the kidneys is the most serious complication of scarlet fever, and therefore everything likely to cause chill and to increase internal congestion must be avoided. Sloughing of the throat occurs in severe cases, and is frequently associated with an enormous brawny swelling of the glands and other tissues of the neck. Efforts to disinfect the throat should be careful and thorough ; it is not likely that the patient can gargle, but the sloughing part must be swabbed or sprayed with glycerin and carbolic or Condy's fluid.

Special attention must be paid to the condition of the skin, and more particularly to that of the hands and feet. The violence of the poison destroys the vitality of the epidermis, and where this is very thick, as in the palms of the hands, the soles of the feet, the fingers, and the toes, it is shed in large masses somewhat resembling a glove or shoe. These peelings are very apt to convey infection ; their separation should be carefully assisted by daily anointing the whole body with a weak carbolised oil or eucalyptus vaseline, and when the peelings separate they should be burnt immediately. The skin of the head also peels to some extent, and therefore not only the comfort of the child but the safety of others is promoted by closely clipping or shaving the hair.

Among the complications of scarlet fever, one of the most important is sloughing or ulceration of the throat. This condition always aggravates the general sepsis and local distress, and should the process eat its way into an artery serious and even fatal hæmorrhage may occur ; but fortunately such cases are rare.

Inflammation of the ear may run high, and in some cases leads to permanent deafness. Relief may be afforded by hot fomentations or bran bags, also by the instillation into the ear of weak carbolised glycerin or a solution of oil of eucalyptus in olive oil (Appendix, Formula 14).

Scarlet fever is frequently accompanied by

what is popularly known as *rheumatism*. There is, of course, no reason why true rheumatism should not be present, but in the majority of cases the painful and swollen condition of the joints is due to the scarlatinal poison. No special treatment is needed, but the ordinary fomentations, or swathing the affected joints in hot wool, will afford some measure of relief.

Inflammation of the kidneys is a very formidable complication of scarlet fever ; it frequently occurs after extremely mild cases which have passed unrecognised, because then no confinement to bed or other treatment has been used to prevent chill ; but it also occurs in very severe cases, where the kidneys, like other organs of the body, are heavily poisoned. The chief symptoms which arouse attention are dropsy and changes in the urine. The urine may become scanty, high coloured, and possibly red or black on account of the presence of blood. In the worst cases the secretion may stop altogether, the child becomes drowsy, and finally comatose. An effort must be made to restore the action of the kidneys by cupping the loins and by means of hot fomentations and hot packs. The disease is, of course, unsuitable for domestic treatment, but domestic remedies are mentioned for the sake of those mothers who most unfortunately cannot secure skilled assistance.

A dark colour of the urine is not always due

to the presence of blood. An excessive use of carbolic acid in anointing the skin may possibly cause carbolic acid poisoning, one symptom of which is a dark green or black discoloration of the urine. This is the reason why a weak solution of carbolic in oil should be used, and alternated with a solution of eucalyptus in oil.

Worms.—After the age of infancy, children are very liable to worms. These are chiefly of three kinds—the *threadworm*, which looks like a minute piece of white cotton, and which is found in and about the anus ; the *roundworm*, which strongly resembles the ordinary earthworm ; and the *tapeworm*, of which there are three varieties, all looking more or less like short snippets of narrow tape or braid joined together to make pieces which may measure several yards.

Treatment of worms.—The *threadworm* may be extirpated by giving daily injections of an infusion of quassia (Appendix, Formula 15); the quantity should vary from 2 oz. in little children up to 4 oz. in adolescents. It should be administered every morning as soon as the bowels have acted, and it should be understood that if the injection is omitted on one day the treatment, which ought to last three months, must begin all over again. It is very important to cure threadworms, because in girls they crawl forward from the anus to the vulva, and even to the vagina, and there cause so much irritation that very injurious habits of scratching, rubbing, and therefore of self-abuse, are likely to follow.

The treatment of *roundworms* consists in the administration of santonin; 2 to 5 grains, with a little white sugar, should be given on an empty stomach three mornings in succession, the third dose being followed by a brisk purge. The success of the treatment is proved if, when a small quantity of fæces is examined by the microscope, no eggs of worms are found.

The eggs of *tapeworms* gain access to the human body through the eating of underdone beef, pork, or fish. The patient should have a very light supper, followed the next morning by a dose of castor oil. Two or three hours later the special draught of extract of male fern (Appendix, Formula 16) must be administered, and after a short interval a small quantity of fluid food may be permitted. If the bowels do not act freely a further aperient dose must be taken, and all motions must be carefully searched for fragments of the worm. The creature holds on to the wall of the bowel by its head, and unless that is dislodged it quickly grows again, and the whole process has to be repeated. The head and the last few segments of the worm are very narrow, and the head itself is difficult of recognition; it is therefore wise to send all the smallest fragments to a pathological laboratory for the verdict of an expert.

PART VI

THE WOMAN IN MIDDLE AGE

Involution. —Just as *evolution* or *development* is the keynote of life from birth to full maturity, and stability the keynote from maturity to the climacteric, so is *involution* the keynote of the years that succeed to this period. The acme of physical development is attained during the early part of adult life—probably between the ages of 20 and 25. Comparatively little difference occurs during the next twenty or twenty-five years, a slight decline in activity and powers of endurance may be noticed, but the woman who enjoys good health and comfortable circumstances ages comparatively little until the time of the menopause arrives.

This great change occurs somewhere about the fiftieth year; the actual time of its accomplishment varies much. As a general rule, the later the function of menstruation was established in youth the earlier is the menopause; thus a woman who commenced menstruating at 17 or 18 may cease at 45 or even earlier; but the woman in whom this function commenced

The Woman in Middle Age

at 11 or 12 will probably continue to menstruate until she is fully 50. It is noteworthy that sexual life, as indicated by the presence of the periods, begins early and ends late in the robust and well developed. It is also to be remarked that the period of active womanhood is longer in those women who make the fullest use of their life, and who use to the best of their ability all their powers of mind and body. The average age of the menopause appears to have risen by at least five years during the last half century.

Changes in the skeleton, organs, and personal appearance. —The changes in the woman's physical nature about the time of the climacteric are not so obvious as are those which occur in the young girl at puberty. There is generally, however, a tendency to the accumulation of unnecessary fat, and this is especially obvious in the face and in the abdominal wall. Few women escape this undesirable increase of adiposity. The fat is also likely to be obvious in parts of the body where it was not much developed during the prime of life; for instance, it will be observed in the tissues covering the ribs, especially those a little below the breast. Not uncommonly the deposit of fat in this position is so great and so well defined that a woman consults a doctor, fearing that she has a tumour.

Some absorption of bony material occurs, and

this is particularly evident in the necks of the thigh bones.ꞌ The heads of these bones are in consequence more nearly at a right angle to the shafts, which slightly diminishes the woman's stature and greatly adds to the chance of a special fracture of the thigh bone which is peculiar to elderly women. The angle of the jaw also alters, its slope becoming more gradual ; consequently the whole curve of the lower jaw is shallower, and this, combined with the absence of teeth, accounted for the so-called "nut-cracker" face which was formerly so typical of the old woman. The very general adoption of well-fitting dentures of artificial teeth has done much not only to preserve the woman's appearance, but also to promote her digestion and general well-being.

The alternative to the deposition of unnecessary fat is an undue thinness and dryness of the tissues which may be specially remarked in the faces and hands of some elderly women.

The changes in the internal organs are less obvious but of far greater importance. As women grow older they notice sooner or later that they are much more easily fatigued, even after comparatively slight exertion, and that they lose their breath badly if they attempt to run or to go upstairs quickly. In some instances this is partly due to anæmia, but it is chiefly due to changes in the heart, the muscles of which

The Woman in Middle Age

may undergo fatty degeneration, or may merely become thinner and flabbier than in the prime of life. The digestive functions are always less vigorous, both because the gastric juice is less potent, and also owing to diminished motility of the whole organism, which, of course, includes the stomach and bowels.

Naturally the organs to show the greatest change after the menopause are those concerned with reproduction. The breasts frequently undergo fatty degeneration, or may become atrophied and pendulous. The womb steadily decreases in size and weight, and its mucous membrane atrophies as its function ceases. Equally marked is the change in the ovaries, which become small, shrivelled bodies in which the ovules are sparse, poorly formed, and evidently degenerate.

Cessation of menstruation.—All the above-mentioned changes are accomplished very gradually, and the disappearance of the function of menstruation may be equally gradual. In the most comfortable and normal cases the amount and frequency of the period become progressively less marked, until from being infrequent and scanty it altogether ceases. Such cases are attended by the least possible disturbance of the general health. In other cases cessation is abrupt, the function having been quite normal and simply disappearing. These women are, if possible, even more fortunate. In a certain number of cases the involution of the period does not proceed so comfortably. Great irregularity, both in amount and time, may be experienced, and sometimes there is a succession of profuse and long-continued losses immediately before final cessation.

Besides the arrest of the periods it is quite normal for the woman to suffer a certain amount of discomfort. There are very frequently tenderness and pricking sensations in the breasts, which are, however, not the seat of any disease. Even more common are certain irregularities connected with the nervous and circulatory systems, generally alluded to as *heats* and *flushes*. Without any warning the woman suddenly feels as if a bucket of hot water had been poured over her head and shoulders; she is hot, red, and sometimes agitated. This uncomfortable condition may be accompanied or succeeded by more or less profuse perspiration. The wisest plan is to ignore these discomforts; they are incidental to the process of the menopause, and the more such nervous discomforts are dwelt on the worse they become. Diminution of diet, absolute abstention from alcohol, and careful regulation of the bowels will mitigate them, but time alone can cure.

Difficulties and dangers of the menopause. — The menopause, like dentition, is a normal process, but it frequently borders on the abnormal. It is a period during which latent weaknesses are likely to become manifest, and old errors in self management may sometimes meet with an appropriate recompense. Among the minor troubles of the menopause must be mentioned certain uncomfortable nervous sensations, such as numbness, irritation, and possibly even pain, in the course of the nerves. These sensations cause great distress because they are thought to portend apoplexy and paralysis, but they are nearly always entirely functional, and only mean that the organism is adapting itself with some difficulty to the altered conditions. To the same category belongs the greater irritability of temper and diminished power of " suffering fools gladly." The whole organism, physical, mental, and moral, is unstable, as it always is during periods of stress and change. If the whole household is not to be disorganised, and if the woman is to retain her self-respect, she must resolutely call up her powers of self-control and learn how to suffer not only in silence but in cheerfulness. After all, in the great majority of cases the minor troubles of the menopause pass away, and the woman who is really sound in body and mind may look forward to many years of health and usefulness undistracted by the constant trouble of menstruation.

During the accomplishment of the menopause, and during the years immediately preceding and following this change, some of the most serious of the diseases of women are apt to occur. There is no need for nervousness, because the great majority of women maintain their health, but every woman should know that hæmorrhage from the vagina, abnormal in quantity or too frequent in time, is a danger signal. The so-called *floodings* may have no graver significance than that they show congestion or other slight abnormality of the mucous membrane of the womb, but they may indicate a peculiar condition of the arteries which permits of too great a loss, or they may be the symptom of fibroid tumours or of cancer. Therefore any woman who has an abnormal discharge should consult her doctor and should request a careful examination. No one, not even a doctor, can guess what is wrong with an internal organ without making an internal examination; and therefore the patient, far from objecting to careful examination, should welcome it. It is only a doctor who can judge aright in such cases and who can suggest the suitable treatment. Most of the lives that are lost owing to internal disease might be saved if only women would recognise the possible gravity of these symptoms and refer the matter to their doctor without loss of time.

PART VII

THE WOMAN IN OLD AGE

How to grow old gracefully.—A simple acceptance of circumstances and of limitations is the
condition of gracefulness at all periods of
life. It is perhaps one of our most difficult and
necessary disciplines that we should always
cheerfully submit ourselves to circumstances and
accept the limitations they impose. Thus the
adolescent girl is graceful when she cheerfully
accepts her rightful position as neophyte and
student; she is not graceful if she eagerly
snatches at the dress, the amusements, and the
duties of adult life. So, too, older women are
not graceful if they disregard the warnings of
their gradually failing powers, and cling with
pathetic but futile tenacity to the dress, the
amusements, aye, and even to the duties, of
former years. Old age may be beautiful, vener-
able, and much beloved, upon condition that
the woman herself thoroughly accepts the new
rôle assigned to her in life's drama. Gradually
she must learn that diaphanous materials and

bright colours do not suit her altered figure and her fading complexion. She must also learn that although artificial teeth are a great blessing, and although a suitable wig may be a charitable covering for a bald head, yet she is committing a sin against her personal appearance as well as against her self-respect if she dyes her hair. Golden hair, and even the comparatively humble brown hair, do not accord in any way with the alteration in her complexion. Nothing is prettier than well-brushed, well-cared-for, grey hair, which lends a softness and refinement to the face, and which, during the period of the Empire, was eagerly coveted by the young and beautiful.

Again, in the matter of amusements and duties, as much and as varied exercise as is compatible with the muscular condition is a means of health, but most athletic games are no longer suitable or enjoyable in the majority of cases. Mercifully the changes in health, strength, and activity develop very gradually, and the woman at 50 years of age is still relatively young and is capable of far more physical exertion than she will be twenty years later. It must also be remembered that " old age " is a very relative term, and that capacity for work and for enjoyment depends not upon the woman's age, but on the elasticity and integrity of her tissues and organs.

The Woman in Old Age

Social value of older women. — The social value of young women consists chiefly in the perfection of their discharge of the duties of wife and mother. The mother in the nursery, and the mother throughout the "noisy years" of the childhood and adolescence of her children, is a person of enormous importance both to her family and to the State. Any illness which cripples her health, any outside occupation which interferes with her primary duties to husband and to children, is a matter of the deepest concern. A young woman who cannot, or will not, discharge these paramount duties is depriving her family and the nation, the present and the future generations, of the benefits which she, and she alone, can offer. It is therefore a real sin when a young married woman refuses to bear a family or neglects the nurture and the welfare of her children, in the pursuit of pleasure, or even in the performance of works which are indeed good, and which ought to be accomplished, but not by her.

At some time in life the burden of the family and the happy yet heavy duties connected with it gradually slip away, and the woman finds herself released, and perhaps somewhat desolate in consequence of release. Her children at school, and her husband busy all day, there is not enough in the management of a well-ordered household to fill her time and to satisfy her energies. In the majority of instances, she is still relatively young and strong, and both her intellectual powers and her moral value are at their best; in short, she is now fitted, both by her own condition and by her circumstances, to contribute her share to the needs of the nation not confined to the domestic sphere. Abundance of work awaits such women; at the present time missionary, philanthropic, municipal, and national necessities cry aloud not only for the technical work to be rendered by younger unmarried women, but also for the inspection, supervision, and administrative work that can best be done by women of greater leisure and maturer years. There is room for everyone, and many departments of useful and happy work can be best filled by women whose experience of life and ripe judgment qualify them very specially for the task.

These activities of women may continue indefinitely, although it is to be hoped that some candid child or sympathetic friend will tell them clearly when the time comes for them to sing their *Nunc Dimittis*, for few things are sadder than to see people clinging to offices which they no longer adorn, and performing with difficulty and inadequacy duties which they formerly discharged with easy efficiency.

Care of their health.—All through life the power of the organism to adapt itself to its

The Woman in Old Age

environment is the measure of its health, its usefulness, and its joy. As a woman grows older she must adapt her activities both of mind and of body to her lessened strength, and her food to her diminished powers of digestion. She will find that certain articles of diet no longer suit her, and these should be avoided. It is not possible that the comparatively inactive body can utilise and dispose of the quantity of food, or the kinds of food, reasonably demanded by those who undergo hard physical work. Probably much less meat should be eaten by all elderly people. Some of them cannot digest uncooked vegetables and fruit, and, contrary to the popular belief, the stronger forms of alcohol are particularly injurious. When the stronger wines and spirits are used as daily beverages the results on the liver, kidneys, and other organs are always bad, and may be disastrous.

As old age creeps on, the power of sleep generally diminishes, or, at any rate, the hours of sleep obtained at night are nearly always curtailed. On the other hand, a tendency to snatches of sleep, or at any rate to drowsiness, is apt to occur at unpropitious moments. As a matter of fact, although the need and the capacity for sleep are diminished, the necessity for rest increases, and care should be taken not to overcrowd the day, nor to overtax failing capacities of mind and body.

The Seven Ages of Woman

Evening shadows and promise of dawn. —
A consideration of the whole course of a woman's
life has led us to believe that each period presents
its own joys, its own difficulties, its own duties
and its own rewards. We have learnt also that
each period of life develops naturally from that
which immediately precedes it, that its beauty,
happiness, and efficiency depend inevitably on
the preparation that has been made for it. We
are therefore irresistibly led to the conclusion
that comfort and happiness in old age can be
secured only by preparation for it by a normal
and beautiful life. As Thomas à Kempis says,
" Thou shalt always rejoice in the evening if
thou hast spent the day virtuously." Further,
we are led to the belief that as the prenatal
months spent in the mother's womb prepare the
infant for a happy or a miserable life after birth,
so doubtless the character and the developed
individuality that we are more or less painfully
forming on this side of the grave is in embryo
the personality that we shall be hereafter. Our
future state may differ from that of the present
as much as the butterfly differs from the grub,
and more than the old woman differs from the
embryo, yet the same individuality will persist,
and we must be throughout eternity the product
of the efforts, aspirations, and prayers of this
mortal life. The prospect is full of hope, and
gives a powerful stimulus to the endeavour of

The Woman in Old Age

every faithful soul to profit to the utmost from
the gifts of heredity, the moulding influence of
environment, and the wonderful blessing afforded
by the providence of God from the cradle to
the grave. Surely, as the Psalmist sings, good-
ness and mercy shall follow us all the days
of our lives, and we shall dwell in the house
of the Lord for ever.

APPENDIX

LIST OF FORMULÆ

FORMULA 1

CASTOR OIL EMULSION

Castor oil	1 ounce
Solution of gum arabic, as much as is necessary to form a milky fluid	
Oil of peppermint . . .	1 drop
Peppermint water . . .	1 ounce

(This is the dose for an adult. Children may take from 2 teaspoonfuls.)

FORMULA 2

OINTMENTS FOR CRACKS AND SORES

(a) Dermatol . . . . . 1 teaspoonful
    White vaseline . . . . 1 ounce
       Mix carefully. Send in collapsible tube.
(b) Iodoform . . . . . 1 teaspoonful
    White vaseline . . . . 1 ounce
       Mix carefully. Send in collapsible tube.
(c) Friar's Balsam, as much as can be rubbed into 1 ounce of zinc ointment
       Send in collapsible tube.

FORMULA 3

OIL ENEMA

Castor oil	3 ounces
Salad oil	3 ounces
One yolk of egg	
Turpentine	1 ounce

Beat all together, warm (by standing bottle in hot water), inject slowly.

Appendix

FORMULA 4
Starch and Opium Enema

Starch or arrowroot	. . .	1 ounce
Laudanum		10 to 15 drops

FORMULA 5
Ointments and Suppositories for Piles

Resinol ointment.
Friar's balsam ointment (Formula 2 (c)).
White precipitate ointment.
Hazeline cream.
Hamamelis suppositories.
Tannic acid suppositories.

FORMULA 6
Magnesium Sulphate Enema

Magnesium sulphate	. . .	1 ounce
Peppermint water	. . .	4 ounces
Warm water	. . . .	5 ounces

FORMULA 7
Ointments for Breasts (Nipples)

See Formula 2.

FORMULA 8
Ointment for Breasts (Nipples)

Cocaine	. . . . .	5 grains
Friar's balsam ointment (Formula 2 (c))		1 ounce

FORMULA 9
Preparation of Milk for Infants *

1st week :—

Milk	. . . . .	1 tablespoonful
Water	. . . . .	2 tablespoonfuls
Lime water	. . . .	1 tablespoonful
Cream (48 per cent.)	. .	1 teaspoonful
Milk sugar	. . . .	½ teaspoonful

Half this quantity to be given as a feed.

* Modified from the " Encyclopedia Medica."

Appendix

2nd to 6th week :—

Milk	2 tablespoonfuls
Water	3 tablespoonfuls
Lime water . . .	1 tablespoonful
Cream (48 per cent.) .	1 teaspoonful
Milk sugar . . .	1 level teaspoonful

6th week to 3rd month :—

Milk	3 tablespoonfuls
Water	3½ tablespoonfuls
Lime water . . .	1 tablespoonful
Cream (48 per cent.) .	1 teaspoonful
Milk sugar . . .	1 level teaspoonful

3 months to 6 months :—

Milk	4 tablespoonfuls
Water	3 tablespoonfuls
Lime water . . .	1 tablespoonful
Cream (48 per cent.) .	1 teaspoonful
Milk sugar . . .	1 level teaspoonful

6th to 8th month :—

Milk	8 tablespoonfuls
Lime water . . .	3 tablespoonfuls
Cream (48 per cent.) .	1 teaspoonful
Milk sugar . . .	1½ teaspoonfuls

8th to 12th month :—

Milk	12 tablespoonfuls
Lime water . . .	2 tablespoonfuls
Cream (48 per cent.) .	1 teaspoonful
Milk sugar . . .	2 teaspoonfuls

FORMULA 10

PASTEURISATION OF MILK

The milk should be kept at a temperature of 155° F. to 165° F. for 20 to 30 minutes. This renders the milk innocuous, so far as pathogenic micro-organisms are concerned ; but, like heating just to the boiling point, or even boiling for two or three minutes, it does not necessarily render the milk " sterile " in the strict sense of the word (" Encyclopedia Medica ").

Appendix

FORMULA 11
Raw Meat Juice

Scrape a quarter of a pound of lean beef into shreds in a cup ; add to this 2 tablespoonfuls of cold water, and leave it, covered with a lid, to stand in a cool place for one hour ; then strain it, and squeeze the juice out of the raw beef through muslin (" Encyclopedia Medica ").

FORMULA 12
Boric-Acid Lotion

Half a teaspoonful of boric acid in a wine-bottle nearly full of hot water. Shake well, then boil, and pour back into the bottle.

FORMULA 13
Friar's Balsam (Special)

Friar's balsam	1 ounce
Rectified spirit	1 ounce

Two teaspoonfuls to each pint or water in bronchitis kettle.

FORMULA 14

Oil of eucalyptus . . .	5 drops
Salad oil	1 ounce

FORMULA 15

A handful of quassia chips
One pint of cold water.
Soak all night. Warm 4 ounces of the infusion, and inject slowly into bowel with a ball syringe.

FORMULA 16

Oil of male fern . . .	1 teaspoonful
Rub up with liquid gum, enough to make a milky fluid	
Add cinnamon or peppermint water	1 ounce

INDEX

Index

Index

Index

Printed by Cassell & Company, Limited, La Belle Sauvage, London, E.C.
F.15.1015

CPSIA information can be obtained at www.ICGtesting.com
Printed in the USA
BVOW05s1024130314

347556BV00011B/214/P